The Temple
I'm Going There Someday

Sharing Time Ideas
2002

by
Susan Luke

Covenant Communications, Inc.

Printed in the United States of America
First Printing: December 2001
07 06 05 04 03 02 01   10 9 8 7 6 5 4 3 2 1

The Temple—I'm Going There Someday: Sharing Time Ideas 2002
Cover Design by Val Chadwick Bagley
Covenant Communications, Inc.
ISBN 1-57734-948-2

Table of Contents

Introduction

What an honor it is to be called to serve in Primary! The responsibility of teaching Heavenly Father's children can be filled with innumerable blessings. It can also filled with innumerable challenges as you try to determine the best way to teach gospel principles. My best advice to you as a Primary leader is to always start your preparations with prayer. Heavenly Father knows the needs of each child in your Primary. He knows their strengths, their weaknesses, their desires. He knows the best way to teach His children. As you earnestly pray for the children in your Primary, the Spirit will guide and direct you in the path you should follow. Although the ideas in this book have been prepared with prayerful thought and consideration, they cannot replace the inspiration you are entitled to as you prepare to teach your Primary children. My hope is that the ideas in this book will complement the inspiration you receive from the Lord. May you enjoy your time spent in Primary serving the youngest members of the Lord's kingdom.

1   I love to see the temple

The temple is a house of God, a place of love and beauty. I can feel the Holy Spirit there.

Activity Overview:

An activity matching various people with their corresponding houses, followed by a panel discussion about the temple.

Preparation:

- Copy, color and cut apart the visuals found on pages 4-7.
- Gather several pictures of temples—including both exterior and interior views.
- Gather "fun-tack" and a chalkboard or display board.
- With the approval of your priesthood leader, invite a few people into Primary to participate on a panel answering questions about the temple. The panel could include a young child who has recently been sealed to his or her parents, a teenager who has participated in baptisms for the dead, and an adult who currently attends the temple.
- Prepare ahead of time several questions that could be asked of the panel. For instance, "What did you do to prepare to attend the temple?", "What kind of feelings did you have in the temple?" or "Why is the temple a place of love and beauty?"
- Prayerfully study Joseph Smith's account of the vision that occurred in the Kirtland temple—D&C 110:1-10.

Lesson:

Place the visuals randomly on the display board. Invite the children to come forward one at a time and match the person or family with their corresponding home. When all matches are complete, direct their attention to the pictures of the Lord and the temple. Read aloud D&C 110:6-8. Discuss why the temple is the house of the Lord. As long as the Lord's people keep His commandments and abstain from polluting His holy house, His spirit will reside there. Display the pictures showing the exterior and interior views of several temples. Discuss the sacred beauty of the Lord's house. Invite the panel members to come forward and encourage the children to ask questions pertaining to the temple. Give help as needed by using the previously prepared questions. Conclude by sharing your testimony of the sacredness of the temple.

 I'll go inside someday to perform sacred ordinances that will prepare me to live with Heavenly Father again. I will make covenants and receive my endowment.

Activity Overview:

The words *ordinance, covenant,* and *endowment* are defined, followed by an activity page to help chlidren learn what they will do inside the doors of the temple.

Preparation:

- Copy the visuals found on pages 8-9—one temple page and one set of doors for each child.
- Prepare to introduce the words *ordinance, covenant,* and *endowment* by making a copy of their definitions found on pages 10-11. Note: By copying all three pages of definitions now (including page 12), you will be ready for additional lessons that follow. You may also elect to keep these definitions on display in the Primary room as a reference throughout the year.
- Gather "fun-tack," chalk, eraser, and chalkboard.
- Gather scissors, glue, optional paper fasteners (two for each child), and crayons.

Lesson:

Place the three definitions on the chalkboard. Explain to the children that the displayed words are special things that take place in the temple. Read aloud the definition for *ordinance*. Share with the children a list of ordinances that are performed in the temple, such as baptism for the dead, eternal marriage, sealing children to parents, and the endowment (which will be defined later in the lesson.) Ask the children if they can think of any other ordinances that take place outside the temple, such as baptism, blessing of children, the sacrament, etc. Read aloud the definition for *covenant*. Ask the children if they can think of a covenant they make with Heavenly Father every Sunday during the sacrament. If they need help, share with them the sacrament prayers found in Moroni 4:3; 5:2, inviting them to listen carefully to the covenants that are made. Read aloud Doctrine and Covenants 82:10 and explain that as long as we keep His commandments, the Lord will always follow through with His promise. Read aloud the definition for *endowment*. Discuss the various kinds of material gifts that the children have received. Compare these material gifts with the sacred spiritual gifts that Heavenly Father bestows upon us. You might invite the older children to look in Doctrine and Covenants 46:10-26 and make a list of some of the gifts that Heavenly Father desires to give to His worthy children. Hand out the previously printed temple pages, doors, crayons to each child. After they have colored the pages, instruct them to cut apart the doors and glue them to the temple page as instructed. Attach the optional paper fasteners as door handles. As the children open the doors, they discover what they will do in the temple.

 I will prepare myself while I am young to go to the temple. I must have a recommend to enter a dedicated temple.

Activity Overview:

The words *recommend* and *dedicate* are defined, followed by a hands-on activity where children make a mobile to take home.

Preparation:

- Copy onto card stock the visuals found on pages 13 and 14—one set for each child.
- Gather scissors, paper punch, crayons, and string for the mobiles.
- Have available a chalkboard, chalk, and eraser.
- If you haven't already done so in the previous lesson, prepare to introduce the words *recommend* and *dedicate* by making a copy of their definitions on pages 11-12.

Lesson:

Introduce the weekly theme and discuss the meanings of the words *recommend* and *dedicate* by using the prepared word strips. Display the word strips in the Primary room. Invite a child to read aloud the monthly scripture (Psalm 24:3-4). Write the words *clean hands* and *pure heart* on the chalkboard. Discuss with the children what it means to have "clean hands and a pure heart." If we use our hands to serve others, does it make them clean? Do we consider our hands to be clean if we use them to break the Word of Wisdom? Are our hearts pure if we strive to think only of wholesome thoughts? Allow the children time to suggest activities that make our hands clean and our hearts pure. Write their suggestions on the chalkboard under the appropriate heading. When finished, pass out the papers, scissors, and crayons. Instruct the children to color and cut apart the mobile pieces by following the heavy outside lines. Punch holes as indicated by the black dots. Using string, hang the heart and hand from the holes at the bottom edge of the mobile. Tie a loop of string through the hole at the top of the mobile. Encourage the children to hang their mobiles so that they will be reminded of the principle learned.

4

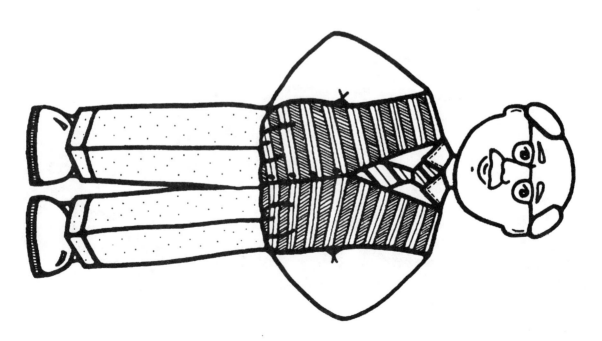

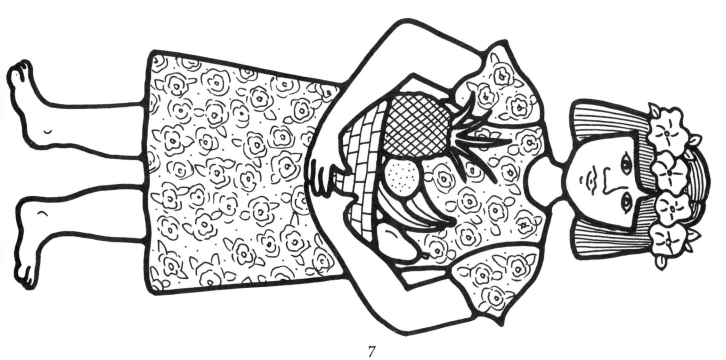

THE TEMPLE
I'M GOING THERE SOMEDAY

to perform sacred
ordinances.

to make covenants
with the Lord.

to receive my
endowment.

Copy one set of doors for each child. (This page contains four sets of doors.) Instruct the children to cut apart their doors and place glue along the backside of the long, gray-colored section of each door. Position each door on the coloring page by matching the gray-colored sections. If desired, paper fasteners can be added to the doors to act as door knobs.

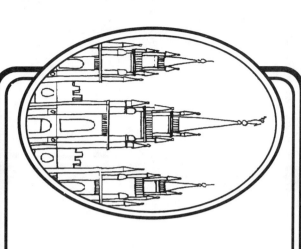

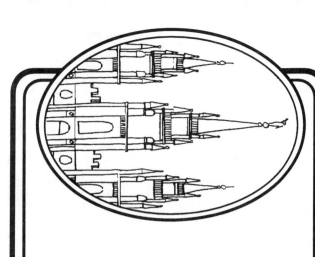

ORDINANCE

A law or commandment from God.

COVENANT

A mutual promise between God and a person or a group of chosen persons.

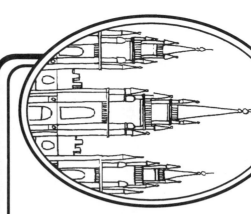

ENDOWMENT

A special spiritual gift or promise given to worthy and faithful Saints.

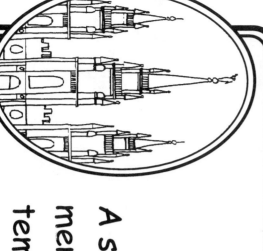

RECOMMEND

A special certificate issued to a worthy church member certifying his worthiness to enter a temple and receive the desired blessings.

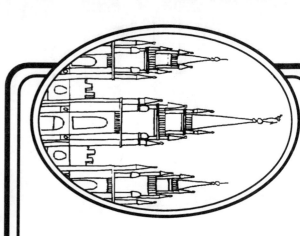

DEDICATE

To give to the Lord through a special prayer for His sacred and holy purposes.

SEALING

An ordinance performed in the temple in which a husband and wife are bound together for time and eternity, and whereby children are bound to their parents.

12

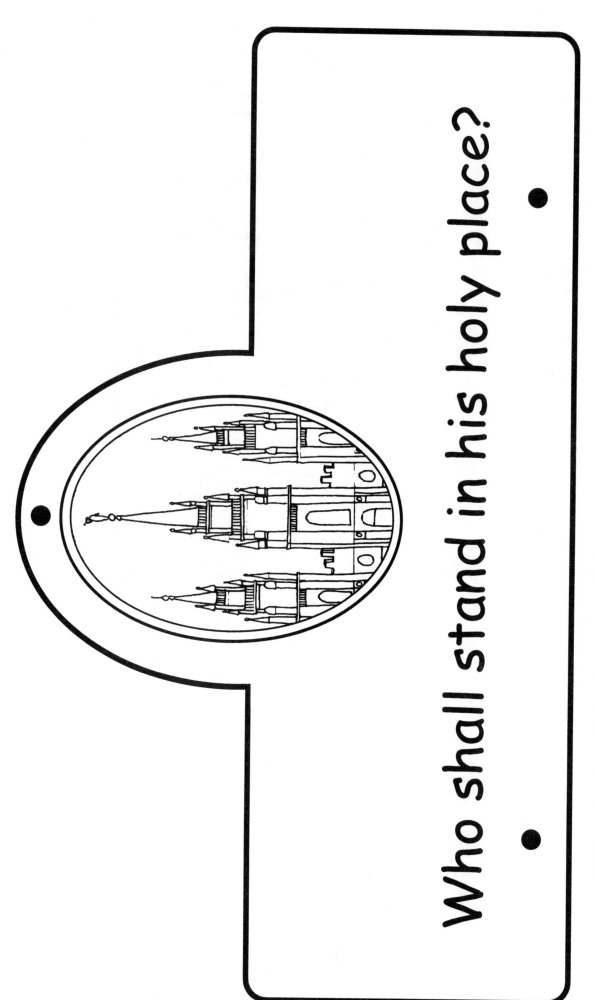

Who shall stand in his holy place?

Using string, hang the heart and hand found on page 14 from the holes along this edge of the mobile.

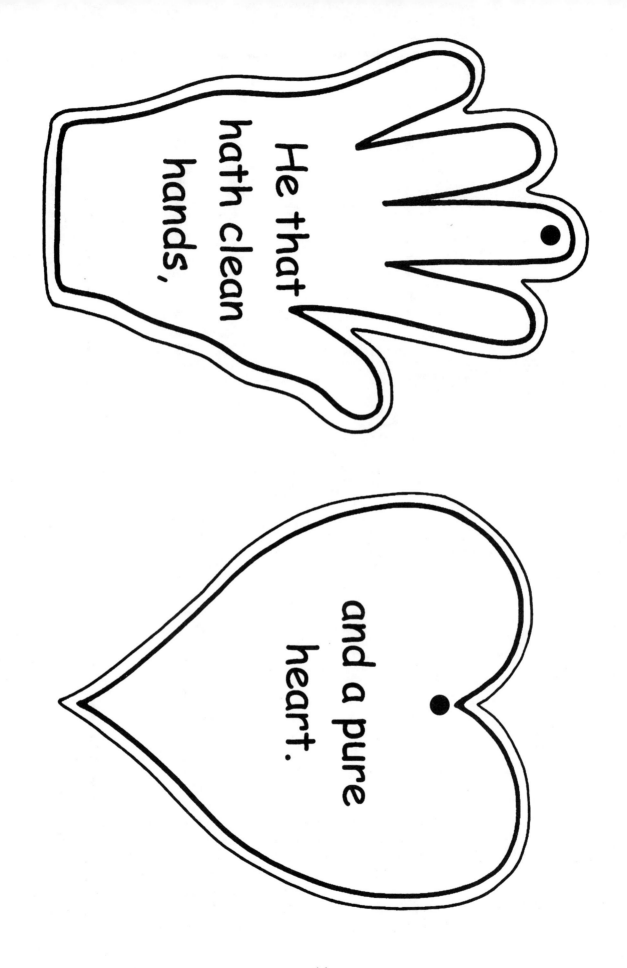

He that
hath clean
hands,

and a pure
heart.

14

2 — *My family can be together forever through the blessings of the temple*

In the temple my family can be sealed together forever. Marriage in the temple is for eternity.

Activity Overview:

The word *sealing* is defined, followed by an object lesson and coloring page where the children draw their family within the outline of a temple.

Preparation:

- Copy the temple picture found on page 18—one copy for each child.
- Gather pencils, crayons, or felt pens for the children to use.
- Gather a variety of pictures showing places where people get married—a park, a church, a house, a boat, a city hall, etc. Be sure to include a picture of a temple. Gather "fun-tack" or tape.
- Cut out a chain of paper dolls that has at least three dolls in the chain. This is accomplished by folding the paper accordian-style and using scissors to cut one half of the doll body keeping the hands connected at the fold. If desired, draw faces on the dolls and label them *Dad, Mom, Child*.
- Gather a clear glass canning jar with a lid.
- If desired, prepare to introduce the word *sealing* by making a copy of its definition found on page 12.

Lesson:

Display the pictures and ask the children which of the pictures represent places where a couple can get married. (All of them.) Next, ask the children which of the pictures represent places where a couple can be married for eternity. (Only the temple.) Introduce the word *sealing* and explain its definition. Demonstrate its meaning by showing the children the paper doll chain and the canning jar. Explain that the doll chain represents a family. This family has been sealed in the temple. Even though members of this family may die, because they are sealed in the temple they will still be together as a family someday. During the explanation, tear each paper doll away from the rest of the chain one at a time and place the doll into the canning jar. When all the family members are in the jar, place the lid on top to seal them together. Explain that just as the jar preserves the paper family and keeps them safe from outside harm, the sealing power of a temple marriage protects and preserves the family. Handout the coloring pages and pencils, crayons, or felt pens. Instruct the children to draw a picture of their family inside the outline of the temple.

Temple ordinances are performed by priesthood authority.

Activity Overview:

An object lesson and discussion about priesthood keys, followed by an activity where the children make their own set of keys depicting priesthood ordinances.

Preparation:

- Copy onto card stock the keys found on pages 19-20—one set for each child.
- Gather scissors, crayons, pipe cleaners, and paper punch.
- Have ready a set of car keys for use during the lesson.
- Prayerfully study information about the priesthood found in the Bible Dictionary (Under the headings *Aaronic Priesthood* and *Melchizedek Priesthood*), Joseph Smith—History 1:68-72, and Doctrine and Covenants 107; 110.

Lesson:

Show the children the set of car keys and ask if anyone can just take any of one of the keys and go out and drive a car. Explain that you not only need the correct key, but that you need a license to drive a car. After meeting certain requirements, such as proper age and ability, the state will issue a license which gives the bearer the authority to drive a car. The priesthood is the authority to act in God's name and operates in a similar manner. Heavenly Father allows male members of His church to hold the priesthood when they reach the age of twelve. They must also meet certain requirements of worthiness. A priesthood holder has the authority or keys to perform God's ordinances on earth. The Aaronic priesthood holds the keys to perform such ordinances as blessing and passing the sacrament. A priest in the Aaronic priesthood can perform baptisms. The Melchizedek priesthood holds the keys to perform temple ordinances. Just as it takes certain keys and authority to drive a car, it takes certain priesthood keys to be given to chosen men to perform the sacred ordinances of the temple. Explain that priesthood keys are not material keys but spiritual keys that unlock the blessings of heaven. Discuss various priesthood holders (prophet, bishop, temple president, priest in young men) and determine what keys they have the authority to use. Hand out the paper keys, scissors, and crayons. After the children have colored and cut apart the keys, punch holes in the keys as indicated and fasten each set together with a ring made from pipe cleaner. The paper keys are labeled to remind the children of the blessings of the priesthood.

My family can live to be worthy of the blessings of the temple. Love grows in my family as we have family home evening, family prayer, and family scripture study, and as we serve one another.

Activity Overview:

An object lesson and discussion on how love grows within a family.

Preparation:

- Copy the hearts found on pages 21-23.
- Gather "fun-tack."
- Gather various objects that portray ways that love grows in a family. For instance, a set of scriptures (scripture study), family home evening manual (family home evening), garden tools (serving in the family), a picture of a family praying (family prayer), etc.
- If desired, bake heart-shaped cookies for the children as a treat.

Lesson:

Display the objects and ask the children to come forward one at a time and choose an object. Ask each child how the chosen object could help love to grow in their family. Beginning with the smallest heart, write the first answer on the heart. For instance, if the child chose the family home evening manual and stated that family home evening helps love to grow within their family, then write *Family Home Evening* on the heart. Place the heart on the display board. Continue the process with the next biggest heart and write *Family Home Evening* plus whatever the next child chooses—maybe *service* or *scripture study*. Continue the process until all the hearts are displayed from smallest to largest with the largest heart containing all the attributes of a loving family. If you baked cookies for the children, hand them out as a reminder of the lesson. You might even suggest they help love to grow by sharing their cookie with another family member.

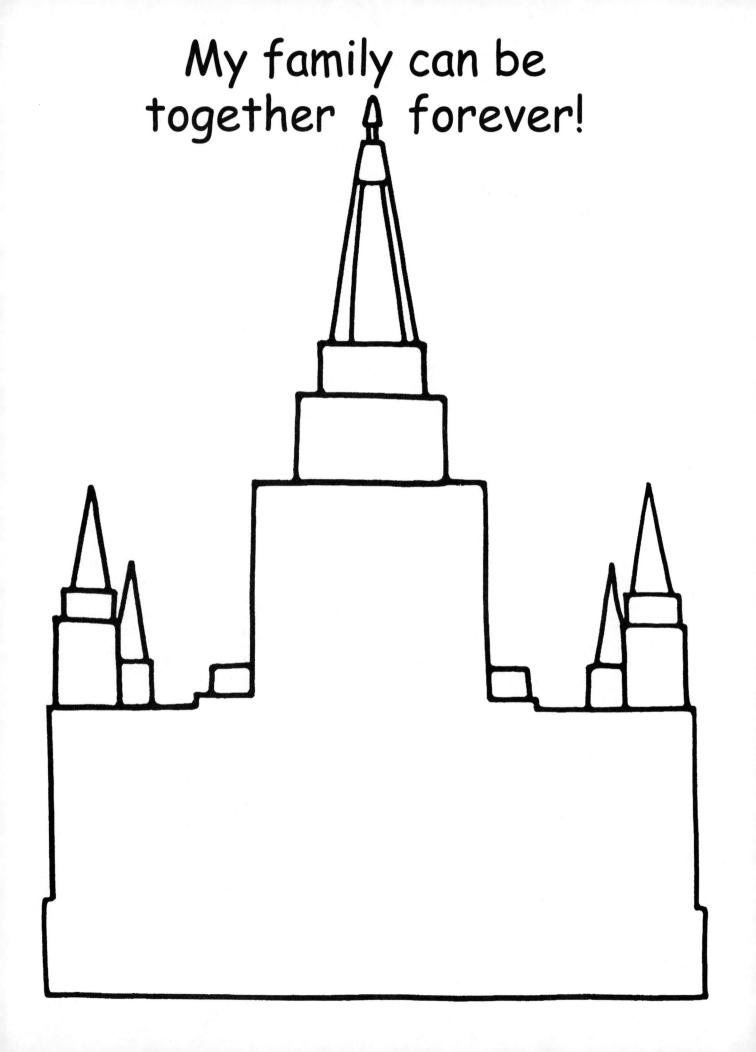

My family can be together forever!

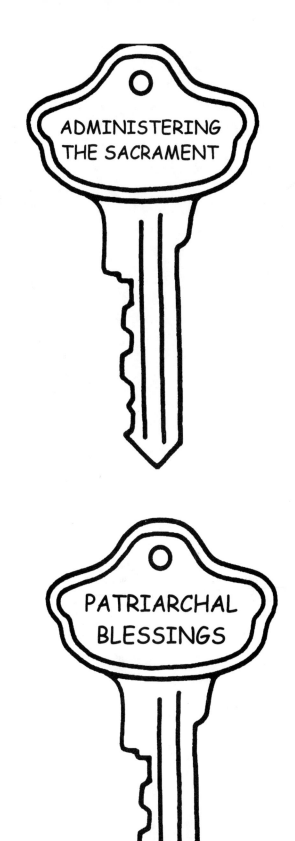

GATHERING OF ISRAEL

ADMINISTERING THE SACRAMENT

ORDINATIONS

PATRIARCHAL BLESSINGS

19

BAPTISM BY IMMERSION

SEALING POWER

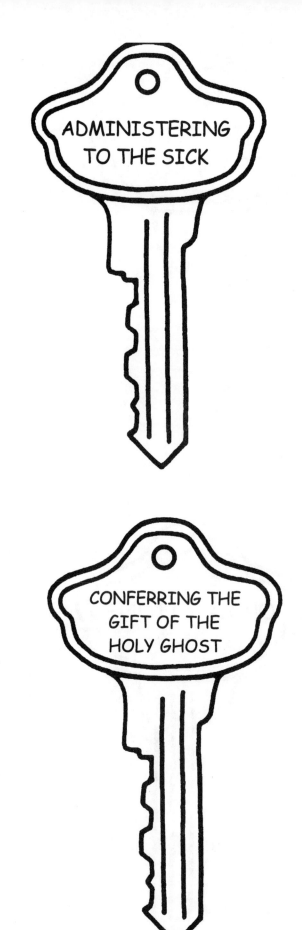

ADMINISTERING TO THE SICK

CONFERRING THE GIFT OF THE HOLY GHOST

20

3   *The temple is the house of the Lord*

When Jesus lived on earth, He came to the temple in Jerusalem.

Activity Overview:

The stories of the baby Jesus being brought to the temple, and the boy Jesus in the temple are told, followed by a hands-on activity where the children make their own pair of turtledoves.

Preparation:

- Copy onto card stock the visuals found on page 27—one set of birds for each child.
- Cut 5″ x 7″ pieces of paper—two for each child.
- Gather crayons, scissors, paper punch, and string.
- Obtain the picture *Boy Jesus in the Temple* (GAK 205).
- Prayerfully study the accounts of the baby Jesus being brought to the temple, and the boy Jesus teaching in the temple found in Luke 2:22-52.

Lesson:

Prior to sharing time, hide the picture *Boy Jesus in the Temple* somewhere in the Primary room. Make two paper birds to be used in the presentation by cutting around the heavy outside line of each bird. Make slits by cutting the line on the body of each bird. Fold two separate 5″ x 7″ pieces of paper lengthwise accordian-style using 1″ pleats. Place a folded piece of paper into the slit of each bird to create the wings. Spread the pleats in the wings as necessary. Punch a hole as indicated on each bird and tie a 15″ string from one bird to the other. By holding the string just off the center, the birds will hang at different levels. Begin the sharing time by retelling the story of Joseph and Mary bringing the baby Jesus to the temple. Show the birds as you tell the story. Explain that the law at the time required a sacrifice to be made to the Lord when a male child was born. Joseph and Mary did not have a lamb sacrifice, so they brought a pair of turtledoves or young pigeons. The sacrifice was showing their obedience to the laws of God and their gratitude for the birth of their son. Continue with the story of Jesus as a young boy of twelve. When you get to the part of the story where Joseph and Mary search for their missing son, have the children look around the room and search for Jesus. Keep searching until someone finds the picture of Jesus in the temple. When recounting this story, be sure to include the correction made in the JST of verse 46. When finished, hand out the papers and help the children make their own pair of birds to remind them of the stories.

After His resurrection, the Savior came to the Nephite temple in the land Bountiful. He taught and blessed the people there.

Activity Overview:

The account of the Savior's visit to the Nephites is told, followed by a discussion and temple-building using paper stones.

Preparation:

- Make seven copies of the temple stones found on page 28.
- Copy the picture of Christ found on page 29.
- Gather "fun-tack," a felt pen, and a display board.
- Obtain pictures that pertain to Christ's visit to the Nephites. (GAK 315, 316, 317, 322).
- Prayerfully study the account of Christ's visit given in 3 Nephi 11-26.

Lesson:

Display the pictures of Christ's visit and share in your own words or by reading selected passages from 3 Nephi the account of the Savior's visit to the Nephites. Be sure to discuss the many things He taught and the blessings that were received by the people. Invite the children to recount the doctrine taught and the blessings received. Write each item mentioned on a separate block and add it to the display board. Use the blocks to build a temple. Build the temple in pyramid fashion beginning with six blocks on the bottom and ending with one block on top. When complete, add the picture of Christ at the top of the temple. At the conclusion, the children could sing *Easter Hosanna*, Children's Songbook, page 68.

When the Savior comes to earth, He often comes to a temple. We can feel His Spirit there.

Activity Overview:

A discussion on making our homes like the temples, followed by a hands-on activity where the children make their own set of door hangers to bring home as a reminder of the lesson.

Preparation:

- Copy onto card stock the door hangers found on pages 30-31—one set for each child.
- Gather scissors, crayons, "fun-tack," and a display board.
- Gather a picture of a temple, house, mountain, school, grocery store,

government building, or other various buildings.
- Read the account of the preparations made by those who wanted to hear King Benjamin's address found in Mosiah 2:5-6.

Lesson:

Place the pictures on the display board and discuss the various purposes of each building or place. Ask which pictures represent a place where the Lord would most likely visit when He comes to earth. If the children haven't picked the picture of the mountain, explain that when the Lord does not have a temple on the earth, He will visit his prophets on the top of a mountain (Moses, Nephi, the brother of Jared, etc.) Our home can also be a temple. Read aloud the preparations that were made by King Benjamin's people. They pitched their tents (homes) with the door opening toward the temple. By doing so, they were able to make their homes an extension of the temple. We live in a time today where even our chapels can be an extension of the temple during a satellite broadcast of a temple dedication. The temple is a sacred place of reverence and beauty. We can feel the Holy Spirit in the temple because no unclean thing is allowed to enter. Our homes can be made to feel like a temple when we show love and respect for each other and prevent unclean things from entering through the television, radio, stereo, or printed material. Read aloud Doctrine and Covenants 88:119 and discuss what kind of house we are to establish and how we can accomplish doing so. Hand out the door hanger, crayons, and scissors. Instruct the children to color and cut apart their door hangers. When complete, the children can hang their door hangers around their house as a reminder to make their home an extension of the temple.

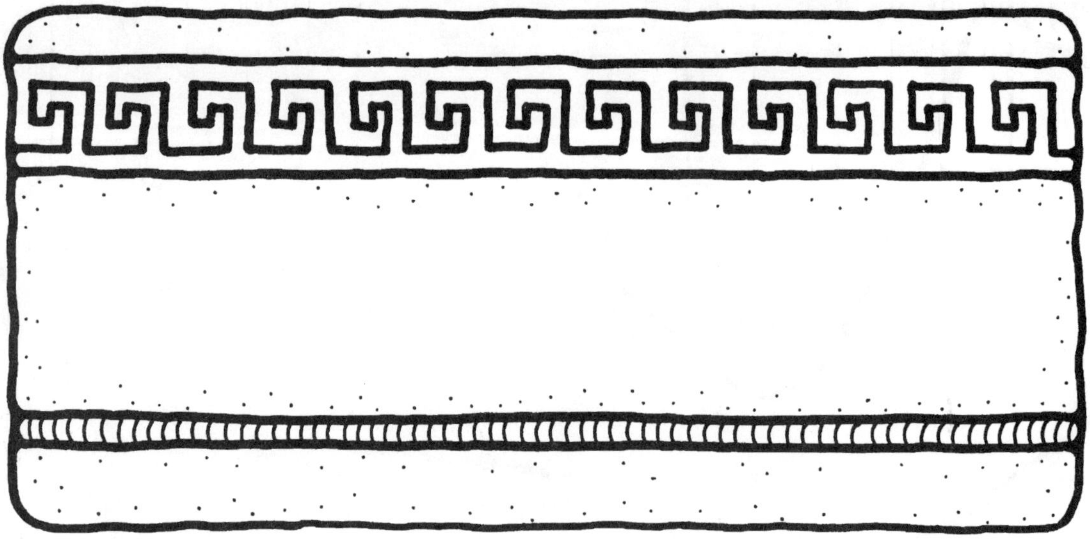

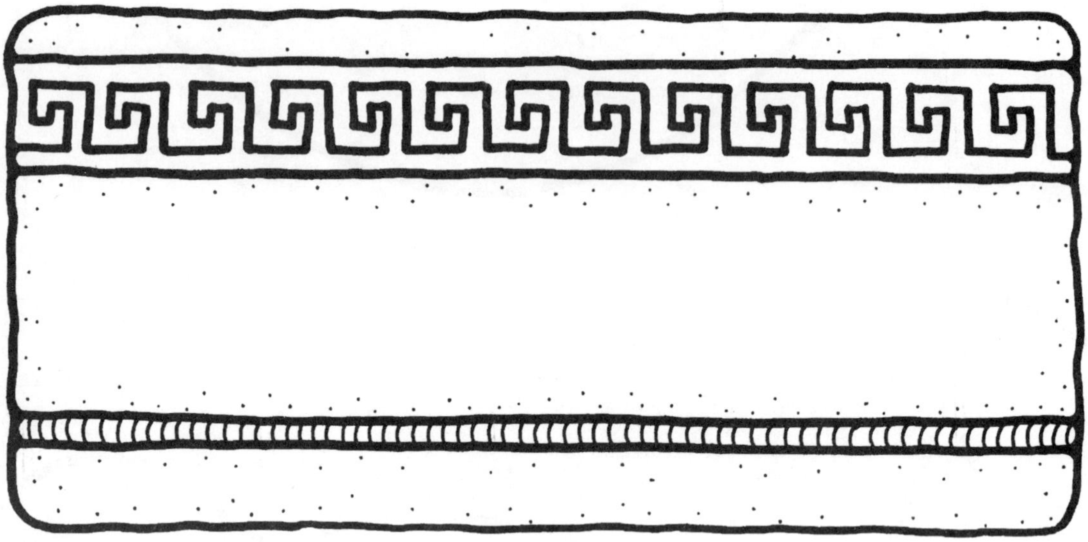

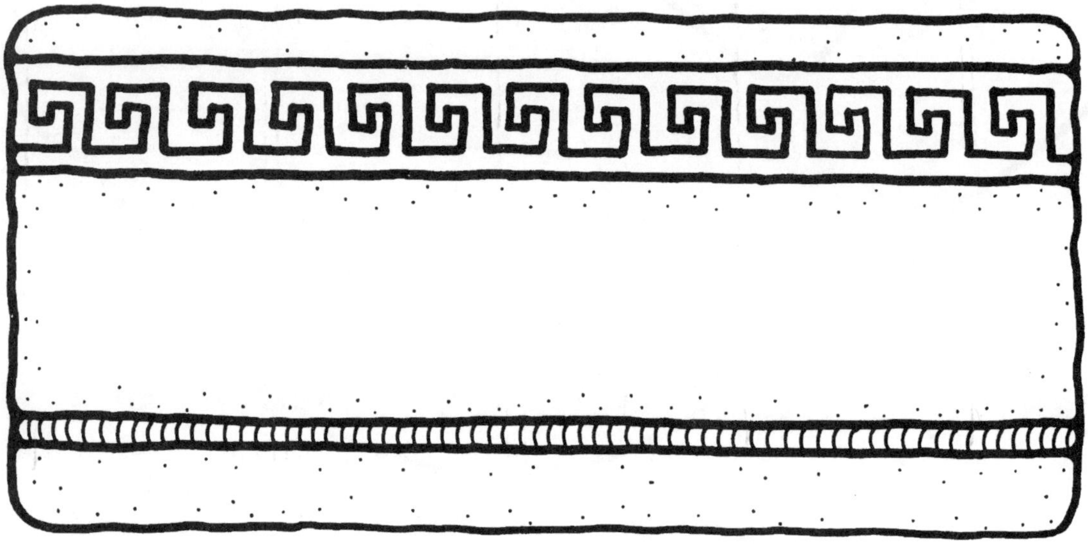

A House
of Prayer

A House
of Fasting

A House
of Faith

A House of Learning

A House of Glory

A House of Order

4 The temple brings the blessings of heaven to earth.

The temple teaches us Heavenly Father's plan of salvation.

Activity Overview:

The plan of salvation is taught through the use of visual aids, followed by the children making their own set of visual aids to be used at home.

Preparation:

- Copy onto card stock the visuals found on pages 35-37. Make one copy to use in Primary, make additional copies for the children to take home.
- Cut apart and color the set to be used in Primary.
- Gather an envelope for each child, "fun-tack," a display board, crayons, and scissors.

Lesson:

Place the visuals on the display board in random order. Explain that Heavenly Father's plan of salvation enables each of us to return to Him if we obey His commandments. The temple teaches us Heavenly Father's plan of salvation. Help the children put the visuals on the display board in the proper order. Discuss the plan of salvation and the fact that Christ is the central figure in the whole plan. Without Christ's Atonement, the plan would not work. Hand out the additional copies along with the crayons, scissors and envelopes. Instruct the children to color and cut apart their own plan of salvation visual aids. Encourage them to place the visuals in their envelopes and take them home to teach the plan of salvation to their families.

The temple is a house of learning and inspiration.

Activity Overview:

An object lesson and discussion about what we learn in the temple, followed by a hands-on activity where children color a picture of their blessings and then "reveal" them through the use of water color paints.

Preparation:

- Obtain a large piece of white, heavy paper, a white crayon, washable watercolor paints (medium to dark in color), water, and a medium-sized paint brush.
- Using the white crayon, write the words of D&C 124:40-41 on the white paper. (During the presentation you will paint over the words. The crayon will resist the paint to reveal what is written.)
- Gather a variety of books that teach different subjects, e.g. math, gardening, sewing, science, cooking, history, etc.
- Obtain a picture of a temple.
- Prepare smaller pieces of white paper, white crayons, and watercolor paints for the children to use.

Lesson:

Prior to Primary, place the white piece of paper over the picture of the temple so that the children will not know that the picture is there. Display the various books. Discuss with the children the many things that can be learned from the various books. Explain the importance of learning and gaining knowledge. Heavenly Father desires for us to gain even greater knowledge. Carefully apply the watercolor paints to the white paper, revealing the writing. Read aloud what is written. Ask the children if they can guess what "house" is to be built to the Lord. After guessing, remove the paper to reveal the picture of the temple. Heavenly Father has commanded us to build temples so that He can continue to reveal many wonderful things that pertain to His gospel. In the temple, we learn more about the plan of salvation, the endowment, and other ordinances. The temple is a place where we can receive inspiration and answers to our personal questions. Hand out the pieces of paper and white crayons to the children. Invite them to draw pictures of blessings they receive because of the temple. Allow the children to carefully paint over their pictures, revealing the blessings they have drawn. Bear testimony that the temple is a house of learning where God reveals His truths to His children.

 A picture of the temple reminds me I am a child of God. If I keep the commandments, I can live with Him someday.

Activity Overview:

A discussion on what it means to be an heir of Heavenly Father, followed by an activity where the Primary leader takes a photograph of each individual child in front of a picture of a temple.

Preparation:

- Copy onto card stock the visual found on page 38—one copy for each child.

- Gather a tall easel and a large, preferably framed, picture of the temple nearest you.
- Obtain a camera and enough film to take an individual picture of each child. Note: The pictures will be taken during this sharing time, then handed out the following week.

Lesson:

Begin by inviting the children to sing "I Am a Child of God," *Children's Songbook*, pg. 2. Of the following titles, ask the children which one best describes Heavenly Father: president, governor, emperor, mayor, or king. After the children choose *king*, write it on the chalkboard. Ask the children to make a list of words that describe a king—giving help as needed. Write their responses on the chalkboard. When finished, discuss how wonderful it must be to be a king. Invite a child to read aloud Romans 8:16-17. Explain to the children what it means to be an heir. As a child of God we have the potential to become like Him and inherit all that He has—even to be a joint-heir with Christ. Explain to the children that in order to do so we must keep His commandments. Show the picture of the temple. Explain that the temple reminds us that we are children of God and we have the potential to become like Him. When we look at the temple, we are reminded that we must be worthy to enter such a sacred house of the Lord. Place the picture on the easel and have the children take turns standing by the temple picture as you take their photograph. After you develop the photos, glue each child's picture in place on the previously copied visuals and prepare to hand them out the following week.

Note: You may want to bring your temple picture and camera the following week in case some of your Primary children were missing the first time.

Death

Final Judgment

Paradise

Spirit Prison

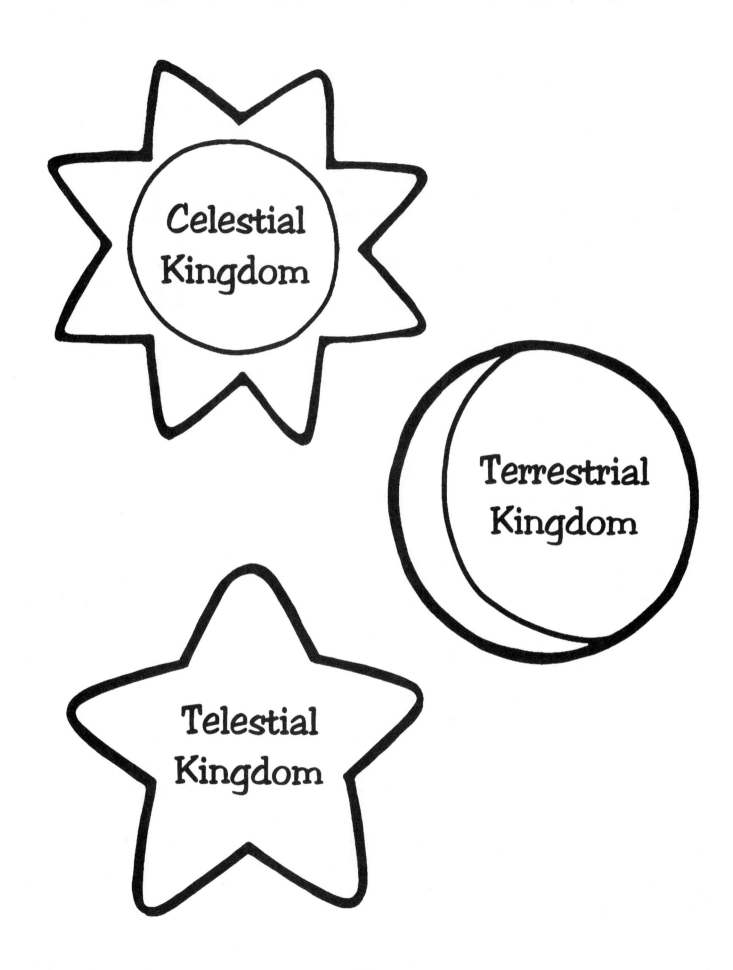

Celestial Kingdom

Terrestrial Kingdom

Telestial Kingdom

I am a child of God.

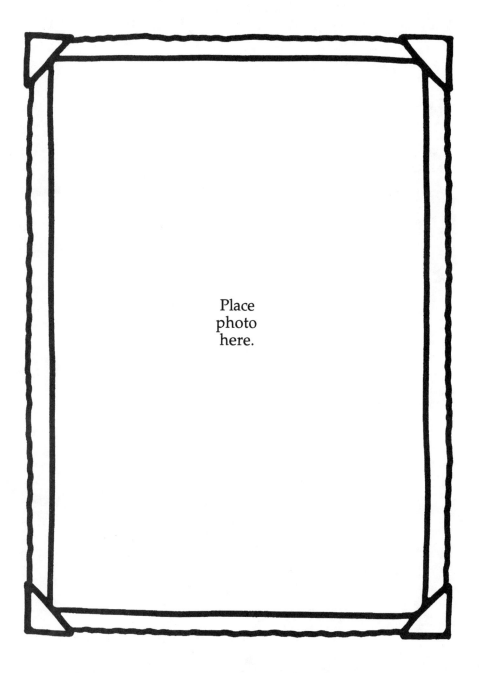

Place
photo
here.

If I keep the commandments, I can live with Him someday.

5

My body is a temple

I will keep my mind and body sacred and pure, and I will not partake of things that are harmful to me.

Activity Overview:

A discussion about the Word of Wisdom including a hunt for "great treasures of knowledge."

Preparation:

- Copy, cut, and color the visuals on pages 42-43. Prior to Primary hide these visuals around the room.
- Obtain a box or chest that can be used as a treasure chest.
- Prayerfully study Doctrine and Covenants 89.

Lesson:

Begin by asking the children if they have ever heard of the Word of Wisdom before. Invite the children to explain in their words what it contains. After the explanations, read aloud the promise found in Doctrine and Covenants 89:18-21. The Lord has promised the Saints who obey the Word of Wisdom will have "great treasures of knowledge, even hidden treasures." Invite a child to come forward and search the room for a hidden treasure of knowledge. When an item is found, read the scripture and discuss its importance. Place the item in the "treasure chest." Continue searching for treasures until all items have been found and discussed. Bear your testimony of the blessings of the Word of Wisdom.

I will only listen to music that is pleasing to Heavenly Father. I will only read and watch things that are pleasing to Heavenly Father.

Activity Overview:

An object lesson and discussion about clean thoughts, followed by an activity where the children's individual silhouettes are drawn and then filled with words and pictures depicting clean thoughts.

Preparation:

- Gather large pieces of white paper—one for each child. Note: Be sure the papers are large enough to accommodate the silhouette of a child's head.
- Gather a pencil, lamp, and crayons.
- Study the following scriptures: Mosiah 4:30; Alma 37:36; and Doctrine and Covenants 121:45.
- Prior to Primary, prepare a large silhouette of a head. Gather several pictures from magazines depicting both positive and negative thoughts and actions. Place the pictures within the silhouette.

Lesson:

Display the previously prepared silhouette. Explain to the children that our bodies are temples and we need to keep them clean inside and out. We cannot allow unclean thoughts that come to us through music, books, television, movies, etc. to enter our minds. Discuss with the children the previously studied scriptures. Explain that Heavenly Father knows all our thoughts and will judge us accordingly. Invite the children to look at the pictures attached to the silhouette. Have them decide which pictures represent thoughts that should be allowed to stay and which ones should be removed. Remove the negative pictures. Invite the children to come forward one at a time and have their silhouette drawn. This is done by attaching a piece of paper to the wall. Position the lamp in a way that when the child stands between it and the wall a shadow of their head is cast onto the paper. Using a pencil or pen, draw around the shadow. When complete, pass out crayons and encourage the children to draw pictures depicting positive thoughts within the silhouettes.

I will use the names of Heavenly Father and Jesus reverently. I will not swear or use crude words.

Activity Overview:

An object lesson and discussion on ways to keep our bodies pure and undefiled.

Preparation:

- Make two copies of the visual on page 44.
- Gather "fun-tack," display board, and a black crayon.

Lesson:

Place the visuals side by side on the middle of the display board. Discuss with the children the importance of treating our bodies like a temple. We would never deface a temple of God by throwing litter on the grounds, placing graffiti on the walls, or running around the grounds shouting swear words. Our bodies should be treated with the same respect we give a temple of God. Read aloud 1 Corinthians 3:16-17. Explain that when we do things to defile our bodies we are making them unclean before the Lord. Direct the children's attention to the visuals on the display board. Invite them to think of things people do and say that defile their bodies. For example, immodest dressing, using swear words, listening to inappropriate music, watching degrading movies, etc. For each thing mentioned, color a part of one of the bodies black and move the body downward on the display board. Continue until the whole body is essentially black and moved to the lowest portion of the display board. When we lower our standards our bodies are unclean and filled with darkness. Compare to the body that is kept clean. Invite the children to list ways that we can keep our bodies clean. This could include reading Church magazines, listening to uplifting music, dressing modestly, using kind words, etc. As each thing is listed, move the uncolored body higher on the display board. Continue until the body is at the upper portion of the display board and there is a great distance between the two. Bear testimony that when we keep our bodies clean and undefiled, we are uplifted and become closer to Heavenly Father.

Shall find great treasures of knowledge

Shall run and not be weary

Shall walk and not faint

The destroying angel shall pass by

42

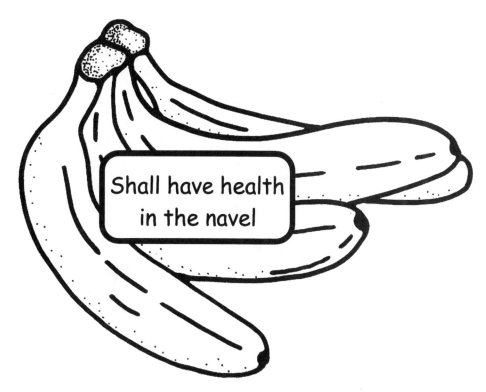

Shall have health
in the navel

Shall have marrow
in the bones

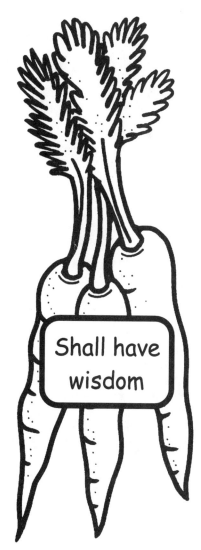

Shall have
wisdom

43

44

6 Temples are a sign of the true church

Moses and the children of Israel had a tabernacle, a temple they carried with them. Solomon built a temple in Jerusalem.

Activity Overview:

An object lesson and discussion on ancient temples.

Preparation:

- Obtain a picture of Solomon's temple and a picture of the tabernacle of the congregation. Note: You might need to use *Moses Calls Aaron to the Ministry*, GAK 108.
- Study Exodus 25:1-8 and gather several items that represent the kind of offerings mentioned in these verses, such as scarves, jewelry, perfume, gold vases, etc.
- Prayerfully study *Temple of Solomon* and *Tabernacle* in the Bible Dictionary.

Lesson:

Display the items that you have previously gathered. Explain to the children that as long as the true church has been on the earth, the Lord has commanded His Saints to build temples. Even Moses and the children of Israel were commanded to build a portable temple while they wandered in the wilderness. It was called the tabernacle of the congregation and enabled the work of the Lord to be carried out among the people. Read aloud to the children the account found in Exodus 25:1-8. Explain that *sanctuary* is another word for temple. The Lord asked the people to make sacrifices and donate their most precious belongings to build His house. Take time viewing and discussing the various kinds of donations made. Ask the children if they think the children of Israel were happy to donate their precious things. To find the answer, invite them to find and read aloud Exodus 33:5-7. The people brought more than enough to build the tabernacle. Ask the children what precious things they would donate today if asked to do so. Would they be as willing as the children of Israel? Display the picture of Solomon's temple and discuss its magnificence. It was patterned after the tabernacle—being exactly double in size. The materials of the temple consisted of gold, silver, iron, copper, timber, and stone. Great care was given to its construction. Bear testimony that just as in ancient times, our temples today are built with the finest materials. Great care is given to make them beautiful houses of the Lord.

The Nephites had temples.

Activity Overview:

A discussion on Nephite temples, followed by an activity worksheet for the children to color and complete.

Preparation:

- Copy the worksheet on page 48—one for each child.
- Gather a pencils and crayons.
- Obtain the following pictures: *King Benjamin Addresses His People*, GAK 307; *Christ Appears to the Nephites*, GAK 315; and *Jesus Blesses the Nephite Children*, GAK 322.
- Prayerfully study Mosiah 2:1-8; 3 Nephi 11:1-17; and 3 Nephi 17:11-25.

Lesson:

Display the pictures you have gathered as you relate in your own words their corresponding scriptural accounts. Explain to the children that Heavenly Father requires His Saints to build temples. Temples are a sign of the true church today just as they were in Nephite time. Heavenly Father's work is carried out in the temples. Hand out the worksheets, pencils, and crayons. Instruct the children to fill in the blanks with answers to the statements at the bottom of the worksheet. The younger children will need help filling in the blanks, but will most likely prefer just to color their page. Encourage the children to follow the last statement and prepare now to attend the temple.

Worksheet Answers:
1. endowment
2. covenant
3. baptism
4. sealed
5. house
6. true
7. now

Joseph Smith restored temple blessings in the latter days.

Activity Overview:

An object lesson and discussion on the restoration of temple blessings.

Preparation:

- Copy onto card stock, color, and cut apart the temple pieces found on pages 49-50.
- Gather "fun-tack" and a display board.
- Prior to Primary, place the pieces of the temple in their proper order on the display board to form a picture of a temple.
- Obtain the pictures *The Prophet Joseph Smith*, GAK 401, *Kirtland Temple*, GAK 500, and *Temple Used Anciently*, GAK 118.

Lesson:

Show the children the picture of the ancient temple. Explain that as long as the true gospel has been on the earth, the Lord has commanded His people to build temples. In these temples, the sacred ordinances required by the Lord could be performed. After the death of Christ, the world fell into a great apostasy, or darkness. Because of the hardened hearts of the people, the truth of the gospel and the ordinances of the temple were distorted and eventually lost. Demonstrate this by moving pieces of the temple to various locations in the room. Display the picture of Joseph Smith. Read aloud Doctrine and Covenants 124:40 and explain that the Lord commanded Joseph Smith to build a temple in the Lord's name and restore the temple blessings to the earth. Display the picture of the Kirtland temple. Explain that to restore means to bring something back to its original state. Joseph Smith did not bring new temple ordinances into the world, but rather brought the ordinances of the temple back to their original state. Demonstrate this by gathering the temple pieces and placing them once again in their proper order. Conclude by bearing testimony of the blessings received from restored temple ordinances.

"The Nephites had temples."

Help build a Nephite temple by filling in the blocks above with answers from the clues below.

1. A special gift or bestowal from God.
2. A mutual promise between a person and God.
3. This ordinance is performed in the temple for the dead.
4. To be bound together for time and all eternity.
5. The temple is the _____ of the Lord.
6. Temples are a sign of the _____ church.
7. When can a person begin to prepare to go to the temple?

49

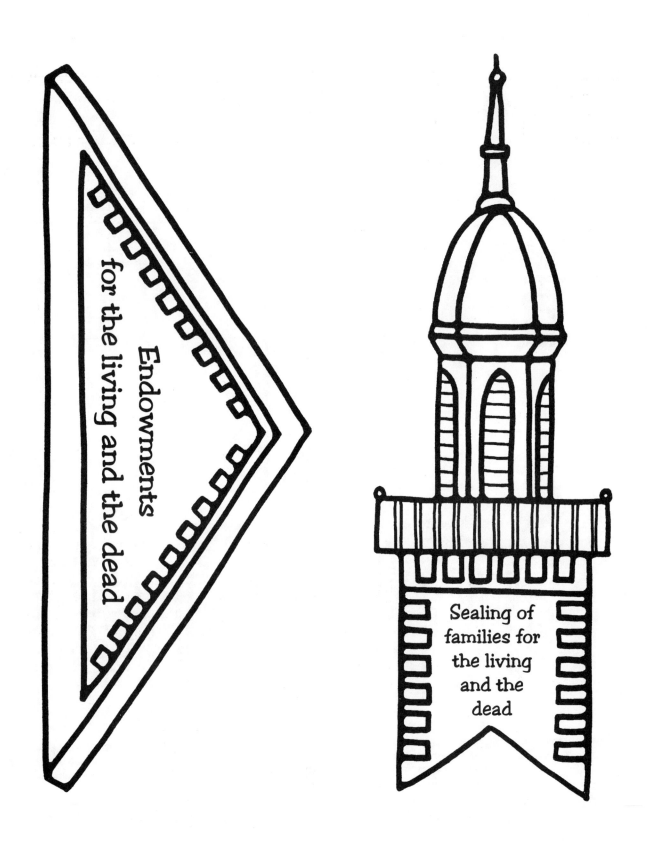

Endowments
for the living and the dead

Sealing of
families for
the living
and the
dead

7

The pioneers worked hard and sacrificed to build temples.

Activity Overview:

A hands-on object lesson to help the children learn of the sacrifices made by the pioneers to build the temple.

Preparation:

- Make a color copy of each of the Kirtland and Nauvoo temples. (GAK 500 and 501). Cut each copied picture into nine puzzle pieces. Number the back of the puzzle pieces with the numbers one through nine.
- Gather "fun-tack" and a display board.

Lesson:

Place the puzzle pieces of the Kirtland temple face down on a table. Without telling the children what temple will be formed from the pieces, explain that as they put the puzzle together they will learn about the hard work and sacrifices made by the early pioneers in building temples to the Lord. Invite the children to come forward one at a time and choose a puzzle piece. Read aloud the corresponding fact as found below. Allow the child to guess what temple is being talked about. Instruct the child to place the puzzle piece on the board. As more pieces are chosen and placed on the board, the children can begin to put the puzzle together. Continue until the children can guess what temple is shown in the picture. Repeat the procedure with the Nauvoo temple. Bear testimony of the great blessings that can be received when sacrifices are made to the Lord.

<u>Kirtland Temple</u>

1. The women of the church kept busy knitting, spinning, and sewing clothing for the temple workmen.

2. Men, women, and children worked very hard to build the temple.

3. Women made curtains and carpets for the temple's interior.

4. Pottery and glassware were crushed and added to the stucco mix to make the exterior walls glisten.

5. Men worked on the temple during the day and then guarded it from the mobs at night.

6. The temple took almost three years to build.

7. Although poverty stricken, the Saints spent from forty to sixty thousand dollars on the temple.

8. Stone was hauled from a quarry two miles south of the temple site, with Joseph Smith serving as foreman of the quarry.

9. One member of the Church, John Tanner, sold his farm in New York to buy supplies for the temple and continued to donate until he had given almost everything he owned.

Nauvoo Temple

1. Men spent one day in ten as "tithing in time" working on the temple.

2. Some workers had no shoes or shirts.

3. The women subscribed one cent per week to buy glass and nails for the temple.

4. One European immigrant donated all the money he had made while serving in the Italian navy—twenty five hundred dollars' worth of gold coins.

5. British Saints raised money to purchase a bell for the tower of the temple.

6. Under heavy persecution from their enemies, the Saints continued to build the temple.

7. Temple clothing had to be handwashed during the night in order to be used the next day in the temple.

8. Approximately five thousand Saints received their endowment before being forced to flee their homes.

9. The temple was dedicated two months after most of the Saints had already left their beautiful city.

Members of the Church today make sacrifices to go to the temple.

Activity Overview:

A discussion and group game that teaches of the sacrifices members of the Church make today in order to attend the temple.

Preparation:

- Copy, color, and cut apart the game pieces found on pages 55-57. (Make two copies of the blank game pieces on page 56.) Using tape or "fun-tack," attach the game pieces to a display board using a pattern of your own choosing—placing several blank game pieces between the pieces with instructions. Note: Be sure to double check the order of the game pieces, making sure the "move ahead" and "move back" spaces don't conflict with each other.
- Copy, color, and cut apart the playing pieces and numbers on page 58. Place the numbers in a container to be drawn from during the game.

Lesson:

Discuss with the children the definition of sacrifice. To sacrifice means to forfeit something highly valued for something that is believed to have a greater value. In Old Testament times, God's people were required to offer burnt sacrifices to Him. This was done to show their gratitude and love for the Lord. We no longer offer burnt sacrifices to the Lord, but offer sacrifices in other ways. In our world today, we value many things such as houses, jobs, our time, material goods, recreational activities, etc. We sacrifice these things in order to attend the temple. Some sacrifices are greater than others. In some cases, people have given up all their material possessions to attend the temple. Others travel great distances, taking many days to reach and attend a temple. Whatever the sacrifice might be, we should do it with a willing heart and a love for Heavenly Father. When we give up that which is valuable to attend the temple, Heavenly Father will bless us with even greater blessings. At the conclusion of the discussion, divide the children into four groups. Give each group a colored playing piece. Instruct the groups to take turns drawing a number from the container and moving their playing piece the appropriate number of spaces, following the directions given on the space. The numbers can be returned to the container. Continue playing until each group has reached the temple.

There is a temple for my part of the world.

Activity Overview:

Preassigned children give a short presentation on a temple, followed by a hands-on activity where the children learn about various temple locations.

Preparation:

- Prior to Primary, gather several pictures of temples. Gather as much information as possible about each of the temples pictured. Give the pictures with information to several children, instructing them to give a short presentation about their assigned temple. Note: The *Deseret News Church Almanac* contains information about each temple.
- Copy onto card stock the visuals found on pages 59-60—one set for each child.
- Gather crayons, scissors, hole punch, and paper fasteners.
- If desired, obtain a globe or world map.

Lesson:

Explain to the children that we live in a time where temples can be found all over the world. Invite the preassigned children to come forward one at a time and give their presentations. Use the globe or world map to show the children where the temples are located. When the presentations are finished, hand out the visuals, crayons, and scissors. Instruct the children to color their worlds, then cut around the thick outside lines. Use the paper punch to punch holes as indicated. Fasten the visuals together by placing a paper fastener through the middle. As the children move the wheel, a temple shows through the window and a star shows through one of the holes indicating where in the world the temple is located.

You stayed home from a slumber party so that your parents could attend the temple. Move ahead two spaces.	You paid your tithing! Move ahead three spaces.	You helped your mom with family history. Move ahead two spaces.
You attended a temple dedication with your family. Move ahead three spaces.	You offered to stay home with your younger siblings so that your older siblings could do baptisms for the dead. Move ahead three spaces.	You sold some of your toys at a yard sale and donated the money to help build temples. Move ahead two spaces.
With your parents, you attended a special fireside about temples. Move ahead one space.	Bonus space. Take another turn!	Bonus space. Take another turn!
You bought candy instead of paying your tithing. Move back three spaces.	When your parents wanted to attend the temple, you complained about having to stay home and babysit. Move back two spaces.	You slept in the day your ward was in charge of cleaning the temple grounds. Move back two spaces.
You stayed home to watch television instead of attending a temple dedication with your family. Move back three spaces.	You complained when you heard your parents were leaving to go to the temple. Move back two spaces.	You didn't come home on time and your parents had to stay home from the temple. Move back two spaces.

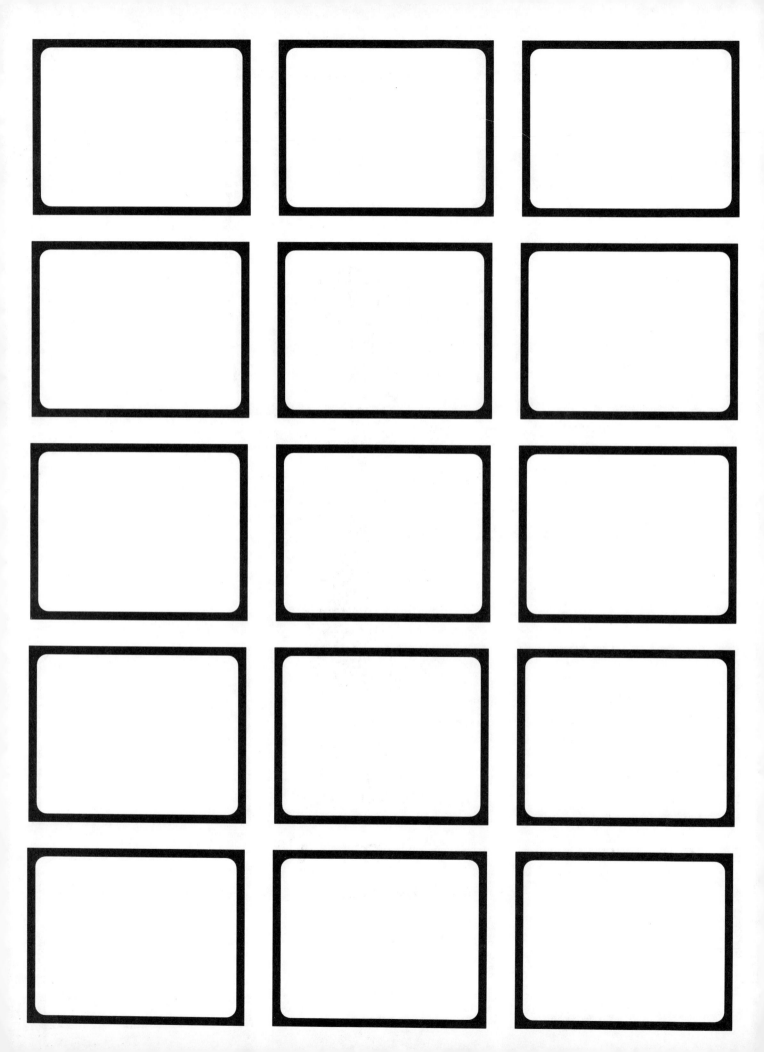

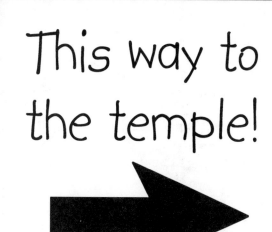

This way to
the temple!

Congratulations!
You made it to
the temple!

58

Temples bless
Heavenly Father's
children throughout
the world today.

Cut along the outside line of the world. Use a paper punch to punch a center hole. Punch out each star. Cut along the outside line of the circle on page 60. Place the world on top of the circle and fasten the two in the center with a paper fastener. As you turn the world, a temple will show through the window, with the location being determined by the star that shows through the corresponding hole.

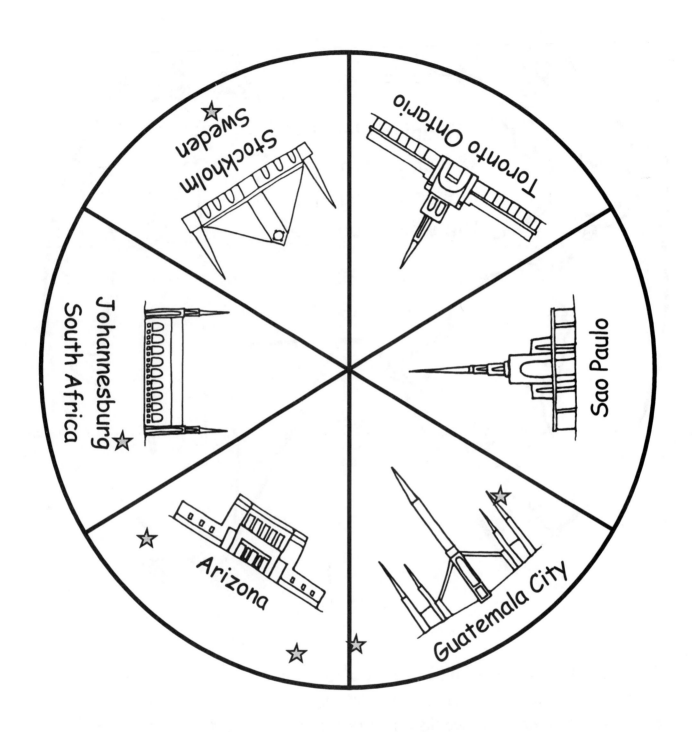

is not applicable.

8   We serve others through temple work

 In the temple, ordinances are performed for our families and others who have died without receiving ordinances such as baptism, endowments, and sealings.

Activity Overview:

An object lesson and discussion on the importance of temple work for the dead, followed by a hands-on activity where the children make a heart-shaped necklace.

Preparation:

- Copy the visuals on page 64—one set of hearts for each child.
- Gather crayons, scissors, glue, a paper punch, and string.
- Obtain a home-canned jar of fruit or other food, an empty canning jar with ring and lid, and several pictures of your current family and your ancestors. Note: The family pictures should be of a size that fits within the empty jar.
- Label the empty jar with *baptism for the dead*, *endowment*, and *sealing*.

Lesson:

Show the children the home-canned jar of food. Ask if they know why people can their food. Explain that canning is a way of preserving food. The canning process seals the food, keeping it together and providing protection from outside influences. Explain that temple ordinances also preserve families, keeping them together and providing protection from outside influences. Show the children the previously labeled jar and pictures you have gathered. Begin by placing your current family picture in the jar. Place the lid securely on the jar. Explain to the children that when a family is sealed in the temple, they are preserved together and protected. Read aloud Malachi 4:6. This scripture teaches us that we should also work to preserve our ancestors. Open the jar and place the pictures of your ancestors into the jar one at a time as you talk about the various ordinances that can be performed for the dead. Note: You may want to relate any personal experiences you have had while doing work for your ancestors. When all the pictures are in the jar, replace the lid and seal it closed. Bear testimony that we can serve our ancestors and preserve their memory by doing their work for them in the temple. To help the children remember the scripture given, hand out the hearts, scissors, and crayons. Instruct the children to color and cut apart their hearts. To make the heart necklaces, fold each heart in half with printed sides facing each other. Open heart #3. Glue the back, left side of heart #2 to the front, left side of heart #1, placing the fold along the center line. Glue the back, right side of heart #4 to the front, right side of heart #1, placing the fold along the center line. Glue heart #3 in place on top of the folded hearts. When finished, it should open like a booklet. Punch holes at the top of the hearts as indicated and tie string to the hearts to form a necklace.

I can prepare to serve in the temple by learning about my ancestors and doing family history work.

Activity Overview:

A guest speaker is invited to give a presentation on family history work, followed by an activity page depicting a family tree.

Preparation:

- Copy the family tree on page 65—one for each child.
- Gather crayons and pencils.
- With approval from your priesthood leader, invite a guest speaker to give a presentation on family history work.

Lesson:

Invite a guest speaker to give a presentation on family history work. This could include personal stories, family heirlooms, and tools used for completing family histories. When finished, hand out the coloring page, pencils, and crayons. Encourage the children to complete their family tree by drawing pictures of their ancestors. If the children can't finish their family tree during Primary, suggest they take them home and ask for help from their family members.

I can write my personal history and write in my journal.

Activity Overview:

A discussion on journal keeping, followed by an activity page and the making of a pencil topper.

Preparation:

- Copy the personal history form on page 66—one for each child.
- Copy onto the card stock the pencil toppers found on page 672—one topper for each child. Note: To save time, you may want to cut out each pencil topper prior to Primary. Cut the slits as indicated by heavy lines on each topper.

- Obtain a sharpened pencil to give to each of the children.
- Gather crayons.
- Locate a variety of appropriate journal entries from pioneers, past ancestors, or your own personal journal to share in Primary.

Lesson:

Begin by sharing some of the journal entries you have gathered. Lead a discussion about the importance of journal keeping. Ask the children what types of things a person could learn from their personal journal entries or the entries of others. Have them try to imagine what it would be like today if the prophets of old had not written down what we have as scripture today. After the discussion, hand out the pencils, pencil toppers, crayons, and personal history forms. Instruct the children to color their topper and place it on their pencil. The children can then use their pencil in filling out their personal history form. Encourage the children to take their form home and use it as starting point if they are not already keeping a journal.

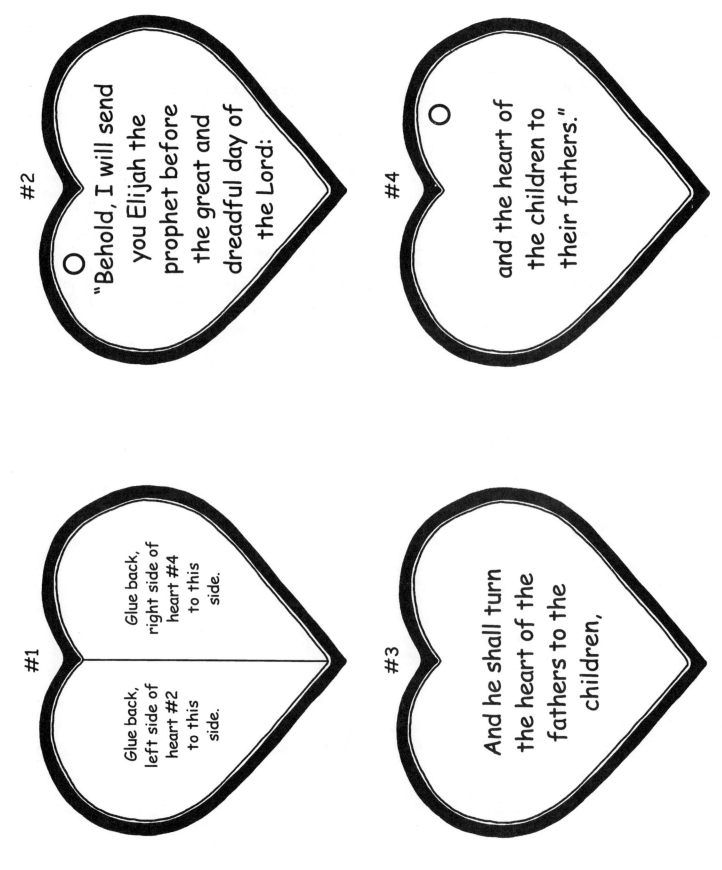

#2

○ "Behold, I will send you Elijah the prophet before the great and dreadful day of the Lord:

#4

○ and the heart of the children to their fathers."

#1

Glue back, left side of heart #2 to this side.

Glue back, right side of heart #4 to this side.

#3

And he shall turn the heart of the fathers to the children,

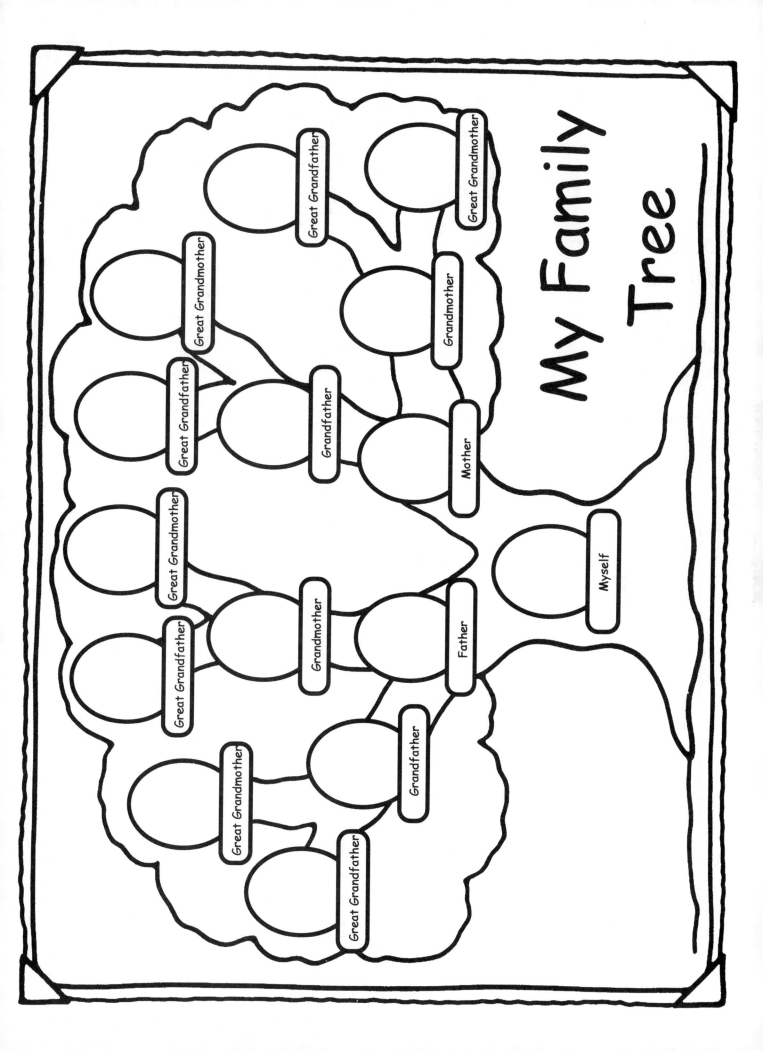

The Daily Journal

A paper all about me!

Someone special is born!

Date of Birth: _____
Where: _____
Weight: _____
Length: _____
Parents: _____

My family!

My family is the greatest because...

_____
_____

My favorite things

Food: _____

Color: _____

Primary song: _____

Sport: _____

Hobbies: _____

Friends: _____

Holiday: _____

Scripture: _____

Future Goals

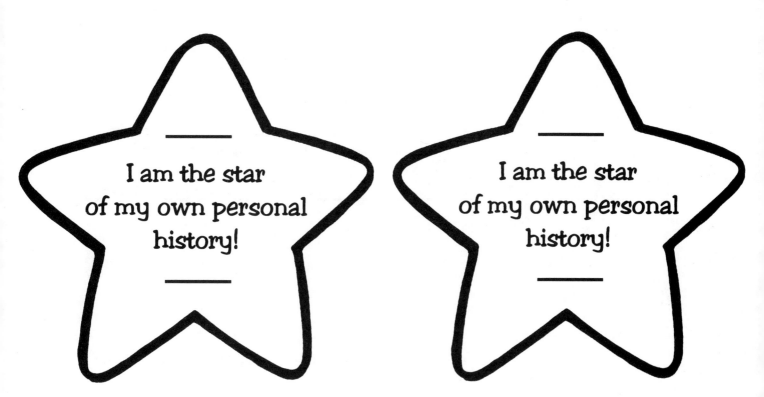

I am the star
of my own personal
history!

I am the star
of my own personal
history!

Copy onto card stock one star for each child. Cut around the outside edge, then cut the two slits in the star. Slide a pencil through the slits.

I am the star
of my own personal
history!

I am the star
of my own personal
history!

9

I will live now to be worthy to go to the temple and serve a mission

I will pay my tithing.

Activity Overview:

A hands-on object lesson about tithing, followed by the making of tithing banks in the shape of a temple.

Preparation:

- Copy onto card stock the tithing bank found on page 73—one for each child.
- Prior to Primary, consult with the bishop or someone else that might know approximately how much the ward spends on various building maintenance, supplies, furniture, etc.
- Gather several tithing slips, tape or "fun-tack," scissors, glue sticks, crayons, chalk, eraser, and chalkboard.
- Prior to Primary, attach tithing slips to several items around the room that are paid for through tithing funds. These include the piano, chairs, pulpit, chalkboard, carpet, pictures, etc. You could also place a tithing slip on the thermostat and light switch to represent heating and lighting costs.

Lesson:

Explain to the children that one of the things they can do to be worthy of temple blessings is to pay their tithing. Direct their attention to the tithing slips placed around the room. Invite the children to come forward one at a time and choose a tithing slip. When chosen, ask the children to guess how much tithing money was probably used to purchase the item for use by ward members. You may want to keep a running total on the chalk board. Continue the process until all the slips have been chosen and discussed. When finished, hand out the tithing banks, crayons, and scissors. Instruct the children to color their bank and cut along the heavy, outside lines. Help the children cut the slit as indicated on the bank. Fold in the flaps and glue, forming a temple-shaped bank for their tithing. Bear your testimony of the importance of being full tithe payers.

I will be honest with Heavenly Father, others, and myself.

Activity Overview:

An activity where groups of children write their own case studies and vote as to whether the person in the study was honest or dishonest.

Preparation:

- Copy the thumbs on page 74—one "thumb" for each group (see lesson below.)
- Be prepared to help the children as needed in writing their various stories of honesty.
- Gather paper and a pencil for each group.

Lesson:

An important part of living worthily is being honest with Heavenly Father and others. Divide the children into groups of 3-4. Give each group a piece of paper, a pencil, and a "thumb" sign. Invite each group to write a short story of someone who is in a situation where they have to choose between honesty and dishonesty. Encourage some of the groups to have the person in their story choose honesty, and the other groups to have the person in their story to choose dishonesty. When each group is finished writing, invite the groups to share their various stories. As each story is told, have the groups give it a "thumbs up" if the person in the story was honest, or a "thumb down" if the person was dishonest. If dishonest, discuss what the person should have done to get a "thumbs up." Continue until all the groups have had a chance to share. Encourage the children to be temple worthy by living an honest life.

I will do those things on the Sabbath that will help me feel close to Heavenly Father.

Activity Overview:

A hands-on object lesson and discussion about Sabbath day activities, followed by the children making heart-shaped pockets filled with word strips depicting appropriate Sabbath day activities.

Preparation:

- Copy onto red colored card stock the heart pocket found on page 75—one pocket for each child.
- Copy the word strips found on page 76—one set of word strips for each child.
- Copy, color, and cut the picture of Heavenly Father found on page 77.

- Copy and cut apart the labels found on pages 78-79. Gather as many pictures as possible that depict the activities listed on the labels. Attach the labels to the pictures.
- Gather scissors, glue sticks, self-adhesive magnetic strips, "fun-tack," and a display board.

Lesson:

Place the picture of Heavenly Father in the center of the display board. Place the remaining pictures and/or labels around the outer edges of the display board, away from the center picture. Explain to the children that Heavenly Father has given us a commandment to keep the Sabbath day holy. The scriptures teach us that we should worship the Lord on the Sabbath day (Doctrine and Covenants 59:10-12). It is also to be a day of rest from our everyday activities. We should only do things on the Sabbath that will bring us closer to Heavenly Father. Invite the children to come forward one at a time and choose a picture or label that depicts a good Sabbath day activity. Have them explain why they chose the picture and then have them place the picture in the center of the display board next to the picture of Heavenly Father. Continue until all appropriate pictures have been chosen and moved to the center. When finished, hand out the hearts, word strips, scissors, and glue sticks. Instruct the children to cut along the heavy, outside line of the heart. Fold the heart pocket, right sides together, as indicated by the dashed lines. Glue the pocket in place. Place a piece of self adhesive magnetic strip on the back of the heart. Instruct the children to cut the word strips apart and place them in the heart pocket. Encourage the children to place the heart pocket on their family's refrigerator. Each Sabbath day can be spent showing love for Heavenly father by following the suggestions written on the word strips.

I will seek good friends and treat others kindly.

Activity Overview:

A hands-on activity lesson demonstrating the importance of good friends.

Preparation:

- Copy, color, and cut apart the visuals found on pages 80-81. Hide these around the room prior to Primary.
- Gather "fun-tack," and a display board.

Lesson:

Explain to the children that we can live now to be worthy of temple blessings by seeking good friends and treating others kindly. Invite the children to seek out the "good friends" that are hidden around the room. When found, invite the children to come forward one at a time and share the good quality possessed by their "friend." Discuss why that particular quality is important in friendship. As each is brought forward and discussed place the friends hand-to-hand on the display board forming one large circle. When the circle is complete, discuss how important it is to have a good circle of friends. When someone in the circle does something, the whole circle of friends is affected. We need to look for the good qualities in others and choose our friends wisely.

I will share the gospel with others.

Activity Overview:

An object lesson and discussion about missionary work, followed by a group game.

Preparation:

- Copy, color, and cut apart the missionary visuals found on page 82. If desired, cover the missionary visuals with clear contact paper.
- Gather 128 pieces of individually wrapped candy. Place the candy in a paper sack.
- Obtain a clear, glass jar just large enough to hold all 128 pieces of candy.
- Gather tape and small round adhesive labels.
- Prior to Primary, create a large circle on the floor by taping the four missionary visuals to the floor, then using the small round adhesive labels to create the outline of the circle between the missionary visuals. (See page 72 for an illustration). Note: Be sure that you have at least one label or visual for each child to stand upon.
- Invite the pianist to be prepared to play a variety of missionary songs from the *Children's Songbook*—starting and stopping several times while the children march around a circle.

Lesson:

Discuss with the children the importance of missionary work and the impact it can have on the number of children that come to Primary. Demonstrate by holding up one piece of candy and explaining that it represents one child. If that child were to go out and invite another child to Primary then you would have two children attending Primary. (Place the two pieces of candy in the jar.) If those to children went out and invited two more children, then you would have four children coming to Primary. (Place two more pieces of candy in the jar.) If those four children went out and each invited a friend, then you would have eight children coming to Primary. (Place four more pieces of candy in the jar.) Continue the process, doubling the amount each time, until you have all 128 pieces of candy in the jar. Explain that just as the jar is full of candy, our Primary could be full of children if we would do our missionary work. Invite the children to stand and take a place on one of the round labels or missionary cutouts that you have placed on the floor. Explain to the children that the pianist will play a variety of songs while they march quietly around the circle. When the music stops, they are to stop. The children that are standing on the missionary cutouts take turns sharing what they can do to prepare to serve a mission or share ways that they can be a missionary now. Continue until most of the children have had a chance to share or until sharing time is over.

My priesthood leaders guide me as I prepare to go to the temple. I will honor my priesthood leaders.

Activity Overview:

The bishop or branch president is invited to share with the children what they can to do prepare to go to the temple, followed by an activity where the children make their own "priesthood" compasses.

Preparation:

- Copy onto card stock the compasses found on page 83—one compass and arrow for each child.
- Gather scissors, crayons, a paper punch, paper fasteners, and string.
- Invite your bishop or branch president to come into sharing time and discuss what the children can do to prepare to go to the temple.
- Obtain a compass and a general understanding of its use.

Lesson:

Begin by showing the compass to the children. Explain to them briefly how it is used and how important it can be in guiding us in the right direction. The Lord has given us righteous priesthood leaders to help guide us to the temple. Invite the bishop or branch president to come forward and share with the children things they can do to prepare for the temple. When finished, hand out the compasses, arrows, scissors, and crayons. After the children have colored and cut out their compass and arrow, attach the arrow by aligning the black dots and placing a paper fastener through both layers. Punch a hole at the top of the compass as indicated by the circle. Tie string to the compass to form a necklace. Encourage the children to look to their righteous priesthood leaders for help and guidance.

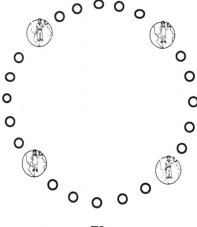

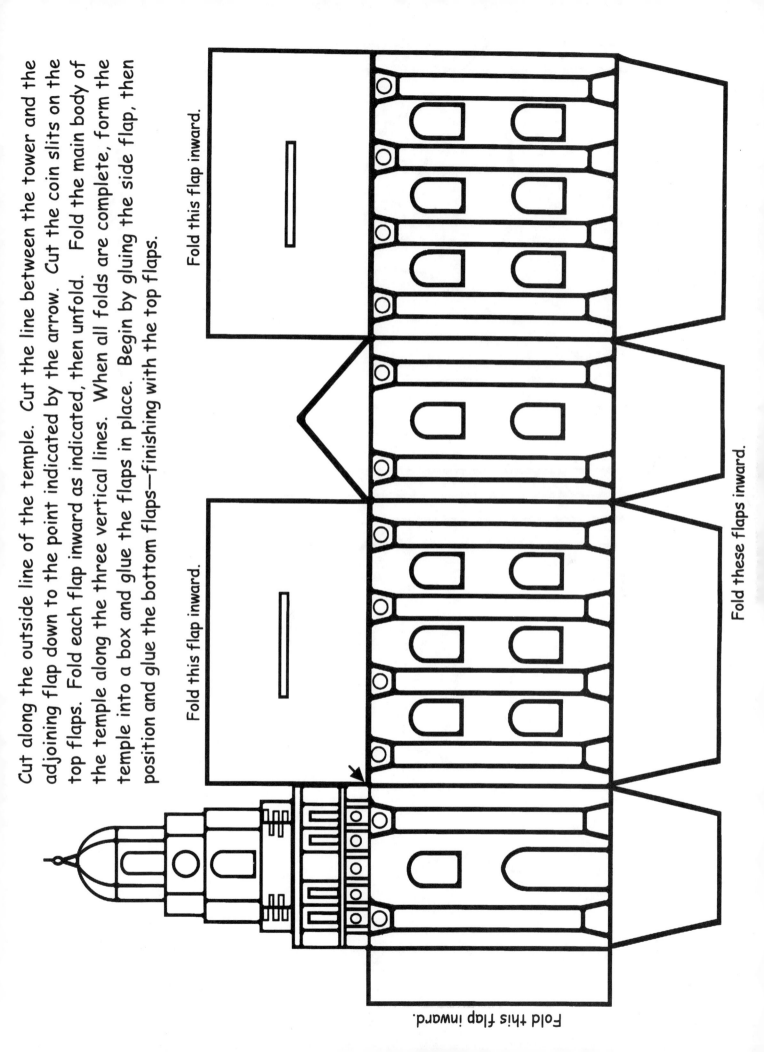

Cut along the outside line of the temple. Cut the line between the tower and the adjoining flap down to the point indicated by the arrow. Cut the coin slits on the top flaps. Fold each flap inward as indicated, then unfold. Fold the main body of the temple along the three vertical lines. When all folds are complete, form the temple into a box and glue the flaps in place. Begin by gluing the side flap, then position and glue the bottom flaps—finishing with the top flaps.

Fold this flap inward.

Fold this flap inward.

Fold these flaps inward.

Fold this flap inward.

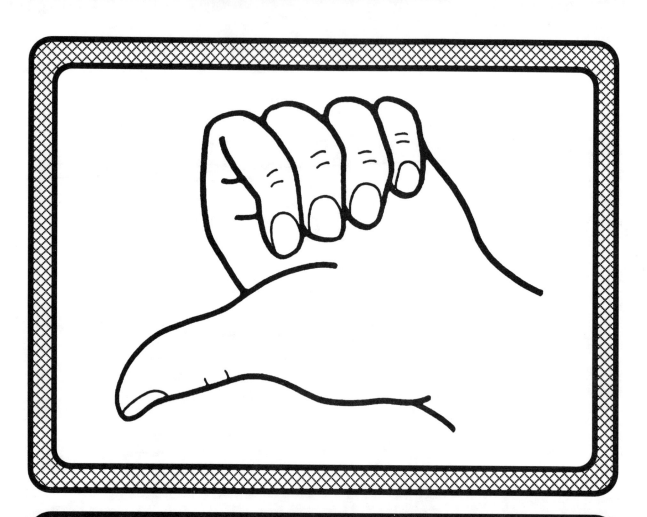

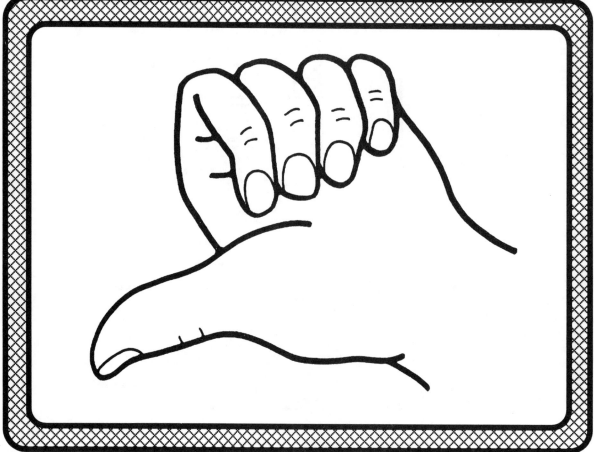

74

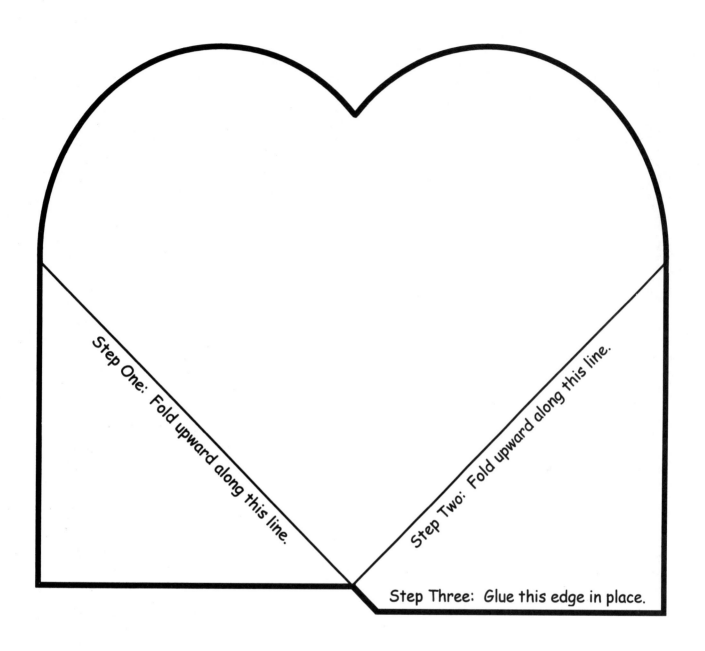

Step One: Fold upward along this line.

Step Two: Fold upward along this line.

Step Three: Glue this edge in place.

I will listen to reverent music.

I will write in my journal.

I will write letters to loved ones.

I will attend all church meetings.

I will read the scriptures.

I will visit the sick and elderly.

I will play quiet games with my family.

I will meditate and pray.

I will serve others.

I will read church magazines.

I will listen to reverent music.

I will write in my journal.

I will write letters to loved ones.

I will attend all church meetings.

I will read the scriptures.

I will visit the sick and elderly.

I will play quiet games with my family.

I will meditate and pray.

I will serve others.

I will read church magazines.

Heavenly

Father

listen to reverent music	take a short nap
write in my journal	play quiet family games
attend church	meditate and pray
study scriptures	write letters
visit the sick	serve others
visit the elderly	read church magazines

shop at the store	listen to loud music
attend the movie theater	work in the yard
watch a sporting event	go boating
go fishing	do unnecessary housework
play at the playground	play sports
watch television	sleep all day

80

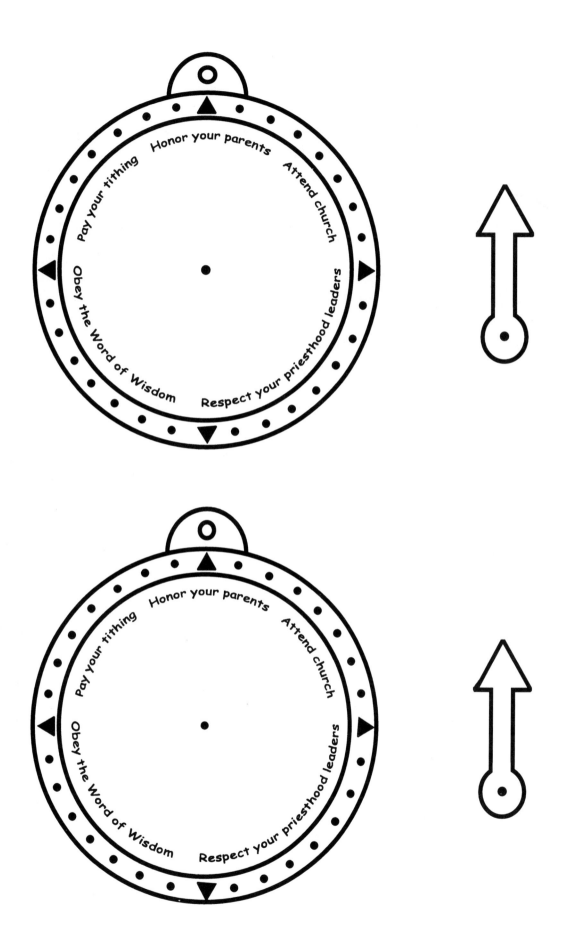

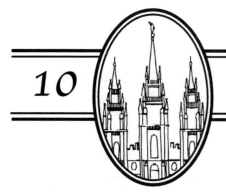

10

*I prepare to go to the temple as I follow
Heavenly Father's plan for me*

I have faith in the Lord Jesus Christ. I will remember my baptismal covenants and listen to the Holy Ghost.

Activity Overview:

An object lesson demonstrating Heavenly Father's plan for our happiness.

Preparation:

- Copy, color, and cut apart the labels found on page 87.
- Place the ingredients listed on page 86 into separate bags or containers and label each with the corresponding label copied from page 87.
- Gather bowls and utensils needed to mix the cookie dough during sharing time.
- Prior to Primary, bake enough cookies to be given out to the children during sharing time. If desired, make the cookies in the shape of a temple.

Lesson:

Explain to the children that Heavenly Father wants us to be happy and has a plan for each us to achieve that happiness. We must follow Heavenly Father's plan exactly to receive His blessings. Compare it to baking cookies. If we want to have great tasting cookies, it is important to follow the recipe exactly. Demonstrate this by mixing the ingredients one at a time as you compare each ingredient to a principle or ordinance of the gospel. Just as following the recipe can result in great cookies, following Heavenly Father's plan can result in the blessings of the temple. Conclude by handing out the previously baked cookies. Bear your testimony of the temple blessings that come to those who follow the Lord's plan.

I will choose the right. I know I can repent when I make a mistake.

Activity Overview:

A hands-on object lesson demonstrating the effects of sin and the blesings of repentance.

Preparation:

- Copy and cut apart the visual on page 88. Glue the two pieces together as indicated. Heavily color the letters with a charcoal pencil, oil pastels, or other art medium that will rub off easily when touched.
- Obtain individually wrapped moist towelettes—one for each child.
- Gather "fun-tack," chalk, an eraser, a chalkboard, and the picture *Jesus Praying in Gethsemane*, GAK 227.

Lesson:

Place the *TEMPTATION* word strip on the chalk board low enough for the children to reach. Discuss what temptations are and invite the children to give some examples of temptations—giving help as needed. Explain that the scriptures teach us that we should "withstand every temptation of the devil" (Alma 37:33). Unfortunately, we sometimes allow ourselves to get too close to temptations. We give into temptations and become unclean through sin. Demonstrate this principle by allowing the children to come forward one at a time and rub their finger on the word strip. The children should all come away with coloring on their finger. (Caution them to avoid wiping their finger on their clothing.) Explain that the coloring on their finger represents a sin or transgression. Since we all sin at some point in our lives, Heavenly Father has provided a way for us to cleansed. Display the picture of Christ in Gethsemane. Share with the children the sacrifice Christ made for us while in the garden—taking upon Himself all our sins if we would repent. Pass out a moist towelette to each of the children with the instructions not to open them just yet. Explain to the children that something inside the packet has the power to clean their finger—but only if we do our part. If we leave the packet untouched, our finger will not get clean. We must have the desire to open the packet and make use of the power it contains. The same is true for the Atonement of Christ. The Atonement is the power that cleanses us of our mistakes. Our part is repentance. The scriptures teach us that "[Christ] suffered these things for all, that they might not suffer if they would repent" (Doctrine and Covenants 19:16). When we do our part and follow the steps of repentance, then the Atonement can take effect and cleanse our lives. Invite the children to open their packets and use the towelette to clean their fingers. Conclude by bearing testimony of the blessings of the Atonement.

 My testimony will grow as I study the scriptures, pray, go to church, and follow the prophet.

Activity Overview:

A matching game depicting ways we can build our testimonies.

Preparation:

- Copy onto card stock two sets of the game cards found on pages 89-90.

Cut apart.
- Gather "fun-tack" and a display board.
- Place the game cards face down on one side of the display board—six rows across, and six rows down.

Lesson:

Explain to the children that we can build our testimony by going to church, reading scriptures, praying, etc. To help them discover ways to build a testimony, invite the children to come forward one at a time and choose a pair of cards. The chosen cards are turned face up. If they don't match, return the cards face down. If they do match, remove the cards and invite the children to place the cards on the other side of the display board—building a temple of their own design. Continue choosing, matching, and placing cards until all have been paired and a temple is built from the cards. In the Logan cornerstone dedication, George Q. Cannon stated, "every foundation stone that is laid for a temple lessens the power of Satan." Through righteous living we can build our testimony upon a solid foundation and lessen the power of Satan in our own lives. Bear your testimony that as we follow God's plan and build our testimonies we will be prepared to attend the temple.

Temple Cookies

3/4 cup shortening
    (part butter or margarine)
1 cup sugar
2 eggs
1/2 tsp. vanilla

2 1/2 cups all-purpose
    flour
1 tsp. baking powder
1 tsp. salt

Mix shortening, sugar, eggs, and vanilla thoroughly. In a separate bowl, measure flour, baking powder, and salt together; blend in. Chill at least one hour.

Heat oven to 400°. Roll dough 1/8" thick on lightly floured board. If available, cut with *temple-shaped cookie cutter. Place on ungreased baking sheet. Bake 6 to 8 minutes, or until cookies are a delicate golden color. Makes about 4 dozen 3" cookies.

*If you can't find an appropriate cookie cutter, you can make a template for a temple from heavy paper, lay it on top of the dough and cut around the edge with a knife. Or, make round cookies wrapped in plastic wrap and decorated with a sticker of a temple.

Copy and cut apart the labels. Attach the labels to the corresponding ingredients by taping, tying with string, or by placing the labels into the plastic bags with the ingredients.

Shortening
is like prayer. An important part of the plan, prayer makes everything smoother in our lives.

Sugar
is like the scriptures, providing the sweet fullness of Heavenly Father's plan.

Eggs
are like faith. Believing in something you can't see, like believing there will be a yoke inside the egg, is the first principle of Heavenly Father's plan.

Vanilla
is like the Holy Ghost. By heeding the promptings of the Spirit, our lives will be flavorful and complete.

Flour
is like baptism. Just as flour provides a firm foundation for the cookie dough, baptism provides a firm foundation of righteousness for us.

Baking powder
is like our testimony. When we bear our testimony to others, it helps our own testimony to rise.

Salt
is like service to others. Sometimes our small acts of service don't seem like much, but if they're missing from the plan, their absence is greatly noticed.

Place glue here.

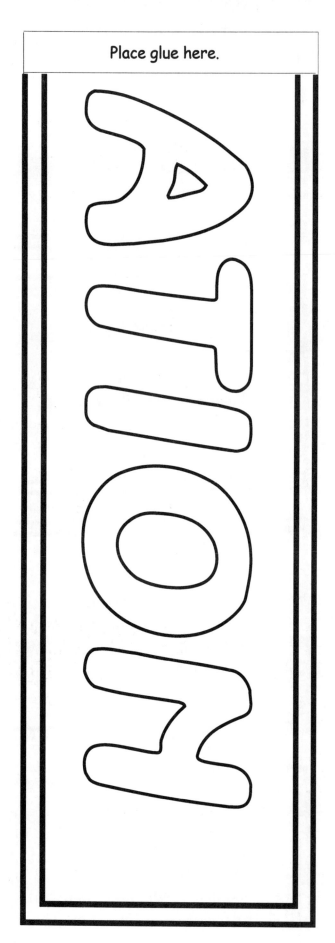

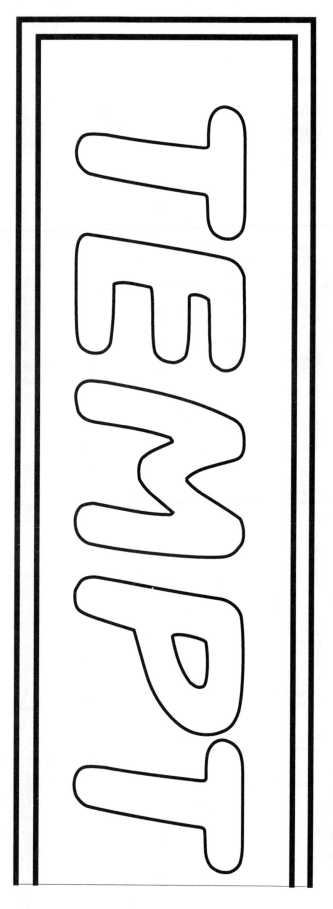

88

church attendance

service to others

listening to hymns

scripture study

fasting

missionary work

daily prayer

paying tithing

journal keeping

temple attendance	forgiving others	reading church magazines
exercising faith	showing gratitude	repentance
attending general conference	sacrificing	attending a baptism

11   *I am thankful for temple blessings*

I am thankful to know that Heavenly Father has a plan for my family to be together.

Activity Overview:

A simple game is played and compared to Heavenly Father giving us directions in our lives, followed by an activity allowing the children to draw their individual family members and seal them together in a plastic sandwich bag.

Preparation:

- Copy the labels found on page 94—one label for each child.
- Gather paper, scissors, pencils, crayons, and one clear, reclosable sandwich bag for each child.
- Prepare to play the game *Simon Says* with the children.

Lesson:

Explain to the children that Heavenly Father has a plan for each of our families to be together eternally. To demonstrate this, invite the children to play the game of *Simon Says*. Play the game for a few minutes until someone reaches "Simon." Instruct the children to return to their seats. Like the game, Heavenly Father gives directions to help us reach our eternal destination. We need to listen carefully and obey each command precisely in order to be successful. In the game, false directions were given to confuse individuals. In real life, the adversary gives false directions to confuse and mislead us. We need to be careful to listen only to Heavenly Father and to shun the adversary. If we follow Heavenly Father's plan, our families can return to live with Him again. When finished with the discussion, hand out the previously gathered supplies along with a label. Instruct the children to draw their individual family members on the piece of paper—keeping in mind that they must fit within the plastic bag. Have them color the label. When finished, instruct the children to cut apart their family members and place them in the bag along with the label, then seal the bag. Be sure the writing on the label shows through the bag. Explain to the children that just as the pictures of their family members are sealed together, we can follow Heavenly Father's plan and be sealed together throughout eternity.

Temple blessings help me feel happiness and peace in my life and in my home.

Activity Overview:

The children create a group mural depicting the blessings in their lives.

Preparation:

- Gather a long roll of white paper, tape or "fun-tack," crayons, felt pens, or other writing utensils.
- Roll out the paper and along the top edge write *"Temple blessings help me feel happiness and peace in my life and in my home."*

Lesson:

Explain to the children that as we live righteously we will be prepared to go the temple and enjoy great blessings by doing so. The scriptures teach "he that doeth the works of righteousness shall receive his reward, even peace in this world, and eternal life in the world to come" (Doctrine and Covenants 59:23). Invite the children to think of temple blessings that bring peace and happiness to them. Roll out the paper and hand out the writing utensils. Encourage the children to create a mural of temple blessings. When finished, display the mural in the Primary room.

Temple blessings help me know that Heavenly Father and Jesus Christ love me. I can show my gratitude to them.

Activity Overview:

A discussion of ways the children show gratitude for Heavenly Father, followed by an activity where the children make their own paper plate pouches. The pouches are then filled with word strips suggesting various ways to show gratitude.

Preparation:

- Copy the visuals on page 95—one set for each child.
- Gather paper plates—one and a half plates for each child.
- Gather glue, crayons, scissors, paper punch, string, stapler, and staples.

Lesson:

Explain that Heavenly Father and Jesus Christ love us so much that They have given us the blessings of the temple. In the temple we have the blessings of learning more about our eternal salvation, helping those who have died without receiving temple blessings, and being sealed for eternity to our families. Heavenly Father is happy when we show Him our gratitude for our many blessings. Using the word strips, discuss with the children ways they can show gratitude for Heavenly Father. When finished, hand out the paper plates, visuals, crayons, and scissors. Instruct the children to color and cut apart the visuals. Place the half plate face down and glue the label along the upper straight edge. Place the whole plate face up and glue the picture of the temple on the top half. Place the half plate face down on top of the whole plate—matching the lower edges. Staple along the lower edge to form a pocket. Cut apart the word strips and place them in the pocket. Punch two holes at the top of the whole plate and add string as a hanger. Encourage the children to show their gratitude for Heavenly Father and Jesus Christ by following the suggestions on the word strips.

I am thankful to know
that Heavenly Father
has a plan for my
family to be together.

I am thankful to know
that Heavenly Father
has a plan for my
family to be together.

I can show my gratitude to Heavenly Father and Jesus Christ.

I will say my prayers each day.

I will be kind to others.

I will be reverent in church.

I will read my scriptures.

I will listen to and obey my parents.

I will be willing to help others.

I will be honest in all that I do.

I will have a cheerful attitude.

12

*When Jesus comes again, He will
come to the temple*

**When the Savior comes again to begin the Millennium, He will come to a
temple.**

Activity Overview:

A review game to test the children's knowledge of the principles learned
over the past year.

Preparation:

- Gather several pictures of temples and *The Second Coming*, GAK 238.
- Gather a display board, "fun-tack," and small treats for the children.
- Prepare ahead of time several questions that review the principles taught
  throughout the year. Some examples could be: What is a covenant?
  What does it mean to dedicate a temple? What can you do to prepare to
  attend the temple some day? By what authority are temple ordinances
  performed?

Lesson:

Prior to Primary attach the pictures of the temples to the display board.
Hide the picture *The Second Coming* behind one of the temple pictures.
Don't let the children know where it is hidden. Explain to the children that
the Savior will come to a temple to begin the Millennium. His coming will
signal the beginning of one thousand years of joy and peace among the
inhabitants of earth. Invite the children to play a game to test their
knowledge of principles they have learned over the year. Invite the
children to come forward one at a time to answer a question. After
answering the question, invite the child to pick a temple they think the
Savior will come to. Lift the chosen picture to see if the picture of Christ is
there. If correct, give the child a small treat. If incorrect, instruct them to
return to their seat as someone else tries to find the picture of Christ. When
the picture is found, you will need to turn the display board around and
hide the picture again. Continue playing until all have had a chance to come
forward. When finished, give a treat to all those who didn't originally
receive one. Conclude with your testimony of the great blessings that the
Second Coming will bring.

We will do temple work in the Millennium. It will be a time of peace and joy and righteousness.

Activity Overview:

A hands-on activity where the children draw pictures depicting what they think the Millennium will be like. These pictures are then added to a heart-shaped poster.

Preparation:

- Copy and cut apart the hearts found on page 99—at least one heart for each child.
- Copy the scripture found on page 100.
- Gather scissors, crayons, pencils, glue stick, and the picture *The Second Coming*, GAK 238.
- Obtain a large piece of paper. Cut the paper into the shape of a heart. Glue the previously copied scripture in the center of the heart. Note: The size of the heart is determined by the size of your Primary. Each child will draw a picture on one of the copied hearts and glue it to the large heart.
- Prayerfully study Moses 7:12-21, 62-65; Doctrine and Covenants 101:22-34; and Isaiah 65:17-25, 11:6-9.

Lesson:

Display the picture of the Second Coming and ask the children to share what they know about that great future event and the Millennium to follow. Explain to the children that many prophets have seen what the conditions will be like during the Millennium. In your own words, share the account of Enoch and his city being lifted up to the Lord—being sure to emphasize verse 18. Enoch saw the millennial day when his city would return to the earth and live in righteousness. The scriptures teach us that the Millennium will be a time of peace and joy. Share with the children the previously studied scriptural accounts. When finished, hand out the hearts, pencils, and crayons. Instruct the children to draw pictures depicting what they think the Millennium will be like. Help the children glue their hearts to the large paper heart. When complete, display the heart in the Primary room. Bear testimony of the great blessings that will come during the Millennium.

 My family and I can prepare for the Savior's coming by living to be worthy of temple blessings.

Activity Overview:

After learning of the parable of the ten virgins, the children are given an activity page to work on at home.

Preparation:

- Copy the lamp found on page 101—one copy for each child.
- Prayerfully study the parable of the ten virgins found in Matthew 25:1-13.

Lesson:

Share the parable with the children and liken it to the Second Coming of Christ. Just as the wise virgins were prepared with plenty of oil to meet the bridegroom, we must be prepared to meet the Savior. Discuss with the children ways they could prepare themselves for the Savior's coming. Hand out the papers. Instruct the children to take their papers home, and every time they complete an act that prepares them for the Second Coming, they are to write it on one of the lines and color the space. Some examples could be reading scriptures, paying tithing, helping others, listening reverently during church, etc. Encourage the children to bring their completed (filled) lamps back to Primary to share with others how they are preparing for Christ's return.

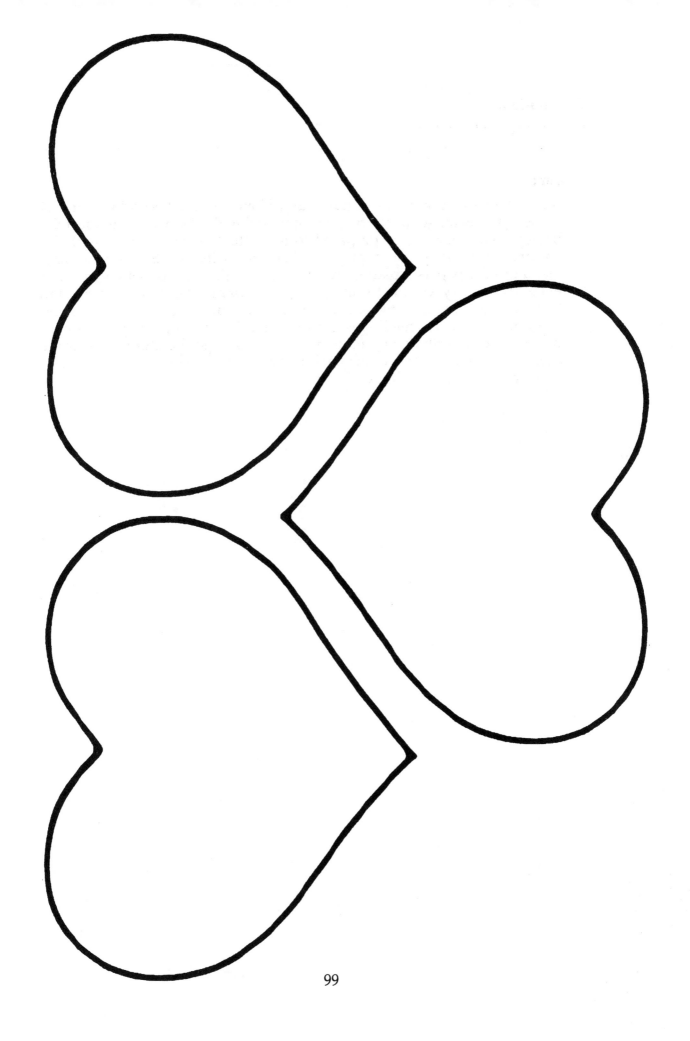

99

"And the Lord called his people Zion, because they were of one heart and one mind, and dwelt in righteousness; and there was no poor among them."

Moses 7:18

My family and I can prepare for the Savior's Coming.

Every time an act is completed that prepares your family for the Second Coming of Christ, write it on one of the lines and color the space.